GUIDE IN THE EXERCISE OF MENTAL PRAYER

VERY REV. JOSEPH SIMLER

CONTENTS

PREFACE

This book was not originally intended to cross the threshold of the religious family for which it was composed. Encouragements on the part of eminent masters, and solicitations of many upright souls, who, as it seems to us, seek God in the simplicity of their hearts, have been for us an indication of the will of Heaven. This is the reason why we publish this new edition, and thus answer without delay the requests that have been addressed to us. This little book will thus truly become the Guide of every man of good will. The experience which it has already undergone proves that the Guide is within the reach of every understanding, and that it is as suitable for seculars, for young men, for fathers and mothers of families, to whom the Christian life is not a vain word, as it is suitable for priests and religious, for pupils in the seminaries, and for the novices in the convents. An abridgment of this Guide, consisting of questions and answers (66 pages, octavo) is called the *Catechism of Mental Prayer*. This substantial resume may be read and even studied to advantage by everyone: it is written in such a style as to be easily committed to memory by novices. We have but one wish to express, and we address it to the Blessed Virgin Mary whom we have saluted, and made known in the 19th Chapter of the Guide, as model and patroness of men of meditation: "Grant, O good and tender Mother, what I ask of thee in the name of thy Immaculate Conception, that all the readers of this Guide may imitate thy example, and may become, in thy school, and under thy auspices, true men of meditation!"

Paris, December 8, 1886,
Feast of the Immaculate Conception of the Blessed Virgin Mary.

1

APPROBATIONS

Letter of Right Rev. Gay, Bishop of Anthedon. To the Very Rev. Joseph Simler, Superior-General of the Society of Mary. Aug. 9, 1886.

Very Rev. Father,

I have read with much interest your *Guide in the Exercise of Mental Prayer*. You have understood how to sum up in this little volume what the most approved authors have taught about this subject, adding thereto, as was but just, the enlightened counsels of the pious Founder of your Institute. To all this you have joined such convincing reasons and such persuasive exhortations for winning souls to the practice of mental prayer that your pages all tend towards increasing the number of these *adorers in spirit and truth,* whom the heavenly Father is ever seeking; for it is always his will that we be saved, and nothing is of greater interest to our salvation than this adoration, of which mental prayer is one of the principal forms.

Not only to your religious family, but, as you desire it, to all souls of good will, your book will prove useful. May God bless your work, and may you be pleased to accept, with my sincere congratulations for the same, the homage of my respect.

+ CHARLES, *Bishop of Anthedon, formerly Coadjutor to Card. Pie, Bishop of Poitiers.*

Letter of Very Rev. E. Grandclaude, Vicar General and Superior of the Theological Seminary of Saint-Dié, Doctor of Divinity and Canon Law. Nov. 15, 1886.

Very Rev. Father Superior,

I have perused with the liveliest interest the work entitled: *Guide of Men of Good Will in the Exercise of Mental Prayer.* Truly, everything in this precious volume, at once brief and complete, calls attention, and merits the approval of all. Doctrine both very precise and exact, nice and methodical divisions, clear, attentive, and unctuous exposition, such are the qualities, which, at the first glance, strike the attentive reader. It is not less noticeable, that the citations are all admirably chosen, and drawn from the most authentic sources; none other than the greatest theological authorities are quoted.

It is hardly necessary to add that the *Guide in the Exercise of Mental Prayer* contrasts strikingly with so many spiritual works published in numbers nowadays, which are as barren in sound doctrine as in the knowledge of the spiritual life.

We therefore consider the Guide as an eminently practical manual, which will safely and agreeably lead men on the paths of mental prayer.

Have the goodness to accept, Very Rev. Father Superior, the expression of my most devoted attachment.

E. GRANDCLAUDE.

Archdiocese of Rennes, Dol & Saint Malo. April 13, 1887.

Very Rev. Father,

On my return from Rome, I find your two little works on mental prayer, and am very grateful to you for this precious gift.

They are such books as are not simply read, but read over and over again. Even after the excellent treatises which have been published on this important subject, these two works of yours make a timely appearance, and will be much relished by religious souls, particularly by priests.

You have prepared, Very Rev. Father, for the good of your readers, an abundant harvest of texts from the masters of the spiritual life, and you will allow me to state that in communing with them you have adopted their language, and your mind has become one with theirs. With all my heart I beseech God to shower his graces upon the Superior of the Society of Mary, upon his devoted Brothers, his books, and all his undertakings.

+ Ch. – Ph. Cardinal Place. *Archbishop of Rennes.*

Archdiocese of Besançon. April 9, 1887.

Very Rev. Father Superior,

I make use of your excellent book: *Guide in the Exercise of Mental Prayer* for my own profit, and find therein qualities of doctrine, precision, and clearness, which the methods known to me fall far short of, indeed. Permit me to congratulate and thank you. Your work deserves a place among the classics bearing on this subject. Written especially for your Brothers, it will be of incontestable utility to all those who take to heart the holy practice of mental prayer. Accept, Very Rev. Father Superior, the assurance of my most affectionate regards.

+ Joseph, *Archbishop of Besançon.*

Archdiocese of Saint-Michel des Rois, (on my Albi pastoral visit). May 6, 1887.

Very Rev. Father,

I thank you for having brought to my knowledge your two little works on mental prayer. The first would deserve a less modest name. It is a complete treatise on this important subject, and it can take a very honorable place by the side of more important works of the same nature. In its simplicity, method, and practical spirit, it possesses a great advantage over several of these works. The second, in its catechetical form, sums it up in an admirable manner; it is a perfect epitome of the whole divine art of mental prayer. I believe both of them are very useful, not only to your novices and religious, but also to seminarians and priests; they will all find precious instructions in your work.

Accept, Very Rev. Father, the assurance of my very humble devotedness.

+ John Emil, *Archbishop of Albi.*

Archdiocese of Touvent. June 18, 1887.

Very Rev. Father,

I received in due time your letter of March 30th last, and the volumes which it so graciously announced to me. First I perused the *Catechism*, and very soon understood the necessity of reading in full the *Guide of the Man of Good Will in the Exercise of Mental Prayer*. The occupations and fatigues of a pastoral visit which has lasted more than two months did not permit a rapid advance in the reading; but this delay gave me a better taste of what I read, and of culling from every page of your excellent work some of the doctrine and piety, which you have so abundantly distributed throughout its pages. You have, Reverend Father, drawn from the best sources, but not without fixing your mark on whatever you have taken from St. Francis, St. Teresa, St. Alphonsus, and other masters of the spiritual life: and your mark is the limpid clearness which distinctly shows the truth, the communicative piety which appeals directly to the heart, moves and fills it with confidence; finally, the wisdom resulting from personal experience. While reading your work, one feels that you have practiced what you teach and that you are entitled to credit. To sum up, Reverend Father, I find your book not only interesting, but also very useful. I will make it my duty to recommend it to all those that come within the sphere of my influence.

Please accept my thanks as well as the respectful sentiments with which I am, Reverend Father,

Your very devoted servant,

+ Joseph, *Archbishop of Bourges.*

Diocese of Saint-Brieuc. April 14, 1887.

Very Rev. Father Superior,

I am very thankful for your kindness in sending me your *Guide of the Man of Good Will in the Exercise of Mental Prayer.*

This Guide deserves recommendation in every respect; it shows a wonderful knowledge of the paths to be followed: it speaks the current tongue; it is within everyone's capacity, without sacrificing a single truth. Happy those who from it will learn to live this interior life, this life of prayer, without which the exercises may, and, to use your own words, do become, in time, so many acts of mere routine, without value and efficacy.

It is especially agreeable to me, Very Rev. Father Superior, to receive from the Society of Mary, for which I bear so great an esteem, a *Guide,* called to effect so much good among souls desirous of learning the art of Mental Prayer.

Accept, Very Rev. Father Superior, with my best thanks my humble attachment in our Lord.

+ EUGENE, *Bishop of Saint-Brieuc.*

Diocese of Beauvais, Noyon & Senlis. April 15, 1887.

Very Rev. Father Superior,

The ceremonies of Holy Week and the solemnity of Easter, as also the confirmations of which I have begun the second series, prevented me from thanking you sooner for your kindness in forwarding to me your excellent work, *The Guide of the Man of Good Will in the Exercise of Mental Prayer*. As yet I could do no more than peruse the table of contents, and to read two or three chapters, but I find that within narrow limits you have skillfully enclosed a quantity of matter and of useful instruction. To this work may be applied what Tertullian said of the Lord's Prayer: *Quantum stringitur verbis, tantum diffunditur sententiis.* I will recommend it to the Directors of the Theological Seminary and to their pupils, who, with the aid of this work, will advance with rapid strides in the art of conversing piously and effectually with God in prayer.

Please accept, Very Rev. Father Superior, with my thanks, the assurance of my most respectful regards in our Lord.

+ Joseph Maxentius, *Bishop of Beauvais.*

Diocese of Versailles. April 21, 1887.

Very Rev. Father,

I thank you for having addressed to me your two little books on mental prayer. From a cursory examination of them, I can say with certainty that they will be very useful and that they are the work of a master in this all-important art of divine contemplation. I should be very glad to see them spread among the clergy and laity of my diocese. For my part, I intend to take them for my spiritual reading for some time, that I may profit by the fruits of your experience.

Please accept with my thanks the expression of my most sympathetic regards in our Lord.

+ Paul, *Bishop of Versailles.*

Diocese of Carcassonne. June 1, 1887.

Very Rev. Father,

You were so kind as to offer me your *Guide in the Exercise of Mental*

Prayer and also the *Catechism* which is a substantial résumé of it. I thank you very sincerely for them.

In placing at the disposal of every soul of good will these two works, originally intended only for your religious family, you have done a good work. Rest assured that you will contribute, in a great measure, to advance perfection, to multiply souls given to prayer, not only in seminaries and in novitiates of the Congregations, but also in the world. Is not this the sole recompense that your spirit craves? It is awaiting you, I doubt not, and I am happy to offer you my congratulations thereto.

Please accept, Very Rev. Father, the assurance of my respectful devotedness in our Lord.

+ Felix Arsenius, *Bishop of Carcassonne.*

Diocese of Fréjus. March 15, 1887.

Very Rev. Father,

His Lordship has perused with the greatest interest the book, — *Guide in the Exercise of Mental Prayer* — a copy of which you have sent to him. His Lordship has charged me to thank you in a particular manner, and to assure you that he will have nothing more at heart than to recommend to his priests and religious congregations your method, which is so substantial, so lucid, and so well adapted to conduct souls in the path of meditation.

Please accept, Very Rev. Father, with the lively and respectful gratitude of his Lordship, the regard of your most humble and obedient servant.

MAILLET, *private secretary.*

Diocese of Lucon. April 19, 1887.

Very Rev. Father,

In the name of the Right Rev. Bishop, I return you thanks for the book—*Guide in the Exercise of Mental Prayer*—which you forwarded to him. Seldom has a spiritual book so captivated me by the profound knowledge of the ways of perfection, by the certainty and extent of the rules laid down, by the simplicity and charm of its style. Your little book is truly the guiding star of the Christian in the pursuit of perfection. His Lordship desires that it be recommended in the Weekly Catholic; we conform to his wishes with pleasure. Please accept, Very Rev. Father, the assurance of my respectful regard.

MARCHEU.

Diocese of Rodez. April 24, 1887.

Very Rev. Father Superior,

His Lordship the Bishop has received your two excellent works on mental prayer. He has charged me to express to you his thanks and sincere congratulations. Though small in volume, the two books contain precious and abundant matter. You have condensed therein the most useful counsels of the masters of the spiritual life, and rendered accessible to all the ways which men ought to seek with the greatest assiduity – those which elevate us to God.

Please accept, Very Rev. Father Superior, the assurance of my very respectful sentiments.

J. TOURZERY, V.G.

2

GUIDE OF THE MAN OF GOOD WILL IN THE EXERCISE OF MENTAL PRAYER. WHAT THE GUIDE PROPOSES TO ITSELF AND TO WHOM IT IS ADDRESSED

1. This guide, dear Reader, offers you its counsels to teach you how to meditate well. It places itself at your disposal, as a faithful and devoted friend, in order at first to initiate you into mental prayer, and to accustom you afterwards to its habitual practice. In its capacity as a *Guide,* it is going, as it were, to take you by the hand, in order to conduct you more surely to this so desirable end.

2. Do not say like so many others: "Why embarrass myself with a guide or method? Has not everyone a mind as well as a heart to pray? Does not God himself say that to find him it suffices to seek him in the simplicity of the heart? Why then should I restrict myself to the numerous directions of an artificial method? Is it even possible to find the way through all the divisions and subdivisions which it indicates?"

3. Doubtless we can pray, and even sometimes make excellent meditations, without having previously studied any method; it is incontestable that simple and upright souls have arrived at the perfection of mental prayer, under the sole guidance of the Holy Spirit; it is even certain that the same thing may be said of meditation as of every art, for instance, of eloquence: that the practice precedes the theory; meditations have been made before there existed any

methods of mental prayer. Many saints have, at first, practiced mental prayer to perfection, and the masters of the spiritual life, after having considered these models, have taught us what to do and the way to take, in order to arrive at the same end.

4. But if, exceptionally, the Holy Spirit has taken it upon himself to direct certain artless souls in the path of meditation, no one should count upon this extraordinary favor. God wishes us to follow the common road, and to have recourse to the natural means, proper to conduct us to this end; to act otherwise would be tempting God.

5. It may unhesitatingly be said that those who despise every method of mental prayer will never become men of meditation. There is a great difference between making meditation in certain circumstances, more or less extraordinary, and making meditation regularly, for instance, a quarter of an hour, a half or whole hour each day.

6. Considered from this point of view, meditation is an exercise similar to all the sciences and arts. I was about to say, to all the professions exercised or cultivated by men; because meditation must be made, not merely when we feel interiorly moved or impelled thereto, but when the hour has come, whatever be then the disposition of our soul, just as we go to perform every other function or duty of our state of life. There is then necessarily an apprenticeship and a teaching of this science; order must be observed and a process adopted; in a word, certain methods must be followed, such as are indicated by nature and experience, which put the soul into the dispositions proper for presenting herself before God, whenever she is invited thereto by the rule or the voice of conscience.

7. Viewed in this light, mental prayer presents the most exact analogy with the exercise of every other art. It forms a whole, a body where every part has its place and reason of being; where all the parts are connected with order and harmony, and afford each other mutual assistance to arrive at a definite result which is in itself the very end of meditation. The method is the ensemble of the rules which lead most easily to this end. It shows the right way, points out the dangers,

removes the obstacles, and directs each one in what he is to do, according to the various circumstances in which he may find himself.

8. The Guide is rather a commentary of various methods than a particular method. It accommodates itself to the method you have already learned and followed until now, and if you are not acquainted with any, it does not require you to learn one before placing yourself under its direction; it suffices, by itself, to conduct you to the end. It purposes to teach you what the Saints and masters of the spiritual life have taught us on the nature, excellence, and advantages of mental prayer; but principally on the means of rendering it accessible and even easy for you, whatever be your age, condition, or intellectual culture. It tends to make you love and esteem this holy exercise, and to cause you to practice it diligently and perseveringly.

9. The doctrine of this Guide has been drawn from the writings and examples of the Saints; we have therefore multiplied the quotations. It has been our chief aim to develop this doctrine of the Saints in a simple manner, by avoiding all that could discourage men of good will and could give to mental prayer the false appearance of an exercise out of reach for the greater number and reserved for a few privileged souls.

10. Behold, why leave aside all that could have the appearance of a scientific method, we present the rules in the form of simple and practical counsels: it is, according to the title, a Guide that offers its services to each one, and says appropriately: "Do that, avoid this, follow that method, take this means, and you will attain the end."

11. On this account also, we lay no stress upon the divisions and nomenclatures generally adopted; the technical terms, the numerous divisions and subdivisions frighten beginners. Nevertheless, we shall employ these terms whenever that which they signify will be explained, in order to show that what at first appeared so complicated is in reality very simple.

12. If this Guide has any distinctive characteristic other than simplicity in the exposition and fidelity to the principles of the Saints, it is the earnestness with which it recommends so frequently the indispensable condition of every good meditation. Which is this

condition, according to the doctrine of our divine Master? It is impossible to be mistaken about it, for it is the one whose necessity and efficacy Our Lord has on all occasions proclaimed: it is Faith.

13. The role of Faith in prayer is extolled by the divine Master with remarkable earnestness and evident complacency: "*Secundum fidem vestram fiat vobis:* According to your faith be it done unto you." (Matt. IX. 29.) "*Magna est fides tua: fiat tibi sicut vis.* Great is thy faith: be it done to thee as thou wilt." (Matt. XV, 28.) "*Omnia possibilia sunt credenti.* If thou canst believe, all things are possible to him that believeth." (Mark IX, 22.) "*Fides tua te salvam fecit.* Thy faith hath made thee safe." (Luke VII, 50.) "*Omnia quæcumque petieritis in oratione credentis, accipietis.* All things whatsoever you shall ask in prayer, believing, you shall receive." (Matt. XXI, 22.) One day, the Apostles, astonished at not having obtained what they desired, asked their Master the cause thereof. "*Propter incredulitatem vestram,* Because of your unbelief", Jesus answered them. "*Amen quippe dico vobis: si habueritis fidem sicut granum sinapis, dicetis monti huic: Transi hinc illuc, et transibit; et nihil impossibile erit vobis.* Amen, I say to you, if you have faith as a grain of mustard-seed, you shall say to this mountain: Remove from hence to yonder place; and it shall remove: and nothing shall be impossible to you." (Matt. XVII, 19.)

14. The Apostles, formed in the school of their divine Master, have in their turn lauded the excellence of faith; but no one has surpassed St. Paul in this, when he enthusiastically relates the wonders operated by faith. (Hebr. XI.) His teaching may be summed up in these words: "Without faith, nothing is done; with faith, nothing is impossible, nothing difficult." To express the bonds which always unite prayer and faith, St. James calls prayer, under any form whatsoever, "prayer of faith, *oratio fidei*." (James V, 15.) Finally, St. Paul, in saying that the just man lives by faith (Hebr. X, 38.), declares to us that all the actions of the supernatural life, amongst which prayer holds the first rank, are essentially acts of faith.

15. There is not a method of mental prayer that speaks of the relation of prayer to faith; but we do not know of any method which lays so special a stress on this truth and places it so much in relief as we

purpose to do. This is precisely the particular end and peculiar mission of this Guide. Father Chaminade (Founder of the Society of Mary, of Paris), whom in preference we have followed in this work, identified the exercise of faith with the exercise of mental prayer, or the spirit of faith with the spirit of mental prayer, or lastly the life of faith with the life of mental prayer, and he was in the habit of calling mental prayer "the prayer of faith."

16. It is then for us a fundamental principle, that in mental prayer, as in justification, *faith* is the *commencement,* the *foundation* and the root. (Council of Trent, Sess. VI, Chap. 8.) Without faith, we cannot approach God, still less enter into relation with him, to speak to him, to listen to his voice, to converse with him. Besides, "prayer under its diverse forms, is at the same time one of the ordinary manifestations and an essential condition of the life of faith; it is, in some way, the breath of the Christian soul. The spirit of faith alone renders continual prayer, and the special exercise commonly called mental prayer, possible." (Const. S. M.)

17. As shown in the title, the Guide offers its counsels to all men of good will. A good will is the only disposition required by the Divine Master of those who present themselves to embrace a life of evangelical perfection. "*Si vis perfectus esse,* if thou wilt be perfect?" (Matt. XIX, 21.); "*si quis vult post me venire,* if any man will come after me." (Matt. XVI, 24.) It is also the only condition required to succeed in the divine art of mental prayer.

18. Everyone receives from God the gift of prayer, because prayer is necessary for salvation; everyone likewise receives from God, to a certain degree, the gift of mental prayer, because meditation, in its essential part, constitutes an inseparable element of every good prayer. (See art. 39.) We say that mental prayer is a *gift* of God, for God always and necessarily does the first part in this act; our cooperation is, however, necessary: it is our duty to improve the gift of God; it depends on our will to render it fruitful. This good will is given to all who ask for it. On this account, the Guide, while declaring that it offers its counsels to men of good will, rejects none who wish to accept them.

19. It is addressed to those upright and generous youths, who have understood that God, their honor, their interest, and conscience cannot be separated, and who have made up their minds to serve God fervently, exclusively, and fearlessly; to Christian mothers, who, after the example of that strong woman in the Gospel, are and wish to remain, with God's grace, the richest, loveliest, and most useful treasure of the domestic hearth; to fathers, who understand that their mission with the children is divine, and that, in order to accomplish it, they must have recourse to the Father of lights, from whom all paternity is derived, and from whom every good gift comes; finally to Christians of every age and condition, to whom their dignity as Christians, as children of God and brothers of Jesus Christ, in this life and in the next, always will be the most beautiful title of glory and nobility. Is it not superfluous to name the religious souls and members of the sacerdotal order, as students of seminaries, clerics and levites of all ranks, priests of the Lord, apostolic men, who, without mental prayer, can neither sanctify themselves nor labor efficaciously at the salvation of souls?

20. Therefore, whoever you may be, whether priest or religious, for whom meditation is a duty and a daily exercise; or a Christian living in the world, for whom mental prayer is necessary, do not forget that it is by the constant fidelity to this duty or exercise, that in reality you will become and remain for all eternity what you are by predestination and by your vocation as Christian, religious, or priest.

21. What progress you would have made until this day, what treasures of sanctity you could have amassed, what good you might have been able to do, in fine, what source of graces you would have found in mental prayer, if you had applied yourself to this exercise as God desired it, if your will had not been on this point out of harmony with God's will? Unhappily, "few souls only understand what God would operate in them, if they would place themselves unreservedly into his hands and allow his grace to act freely." (St. Ignatius.)

22. I address myself, therefore, to you, my dear friend, who are listening in this moment to your Guide, and I give this joyful assur-

ance! You will become a man of mental prayer if you never cease to *will* it.

23. It is never too late to commence, but it is always urgent to give oneself to it. How many saints have succeeded to perfection in this heavenly art, some after years which they passed in enmity with God; others who were not prepared by long instructions and high intellectual culture, such as the solitaries of the desert, St. Francis of Assisi, and many of his first disciples.

24. You will not fail to draw the conclusion which follows from this doctrine and these examples, and you will say to yourself: "I shall become a man of meditation, because I will it; and by meditation I shall enter definitively on the way which leads to the perfection of my holy vocation."

25. In what follows, there will be question of that kind of meditation only, in which every one can succeed. The other kinds are reserved for souls whom God calls individually thereto; it would be rashness for anyone to adopt them of his own accord. "We ought," says St. Vincent de Paul, "to honor this kind of sublime meditations, these unions, these passive contemplations, which some persons have taught and which are practiced by souls chosen and conducted by God himself in paths trodden by but few. Still, these meditations, so perfect in appearance, are not always very secure. We must therefore apply ourselves to a more simple and humble manner of praying, until the Holy Spirit shall himself raise us to a higher contemplation."

3

IN WHAT PRAYER ESSENTIALLY CONSISTS. WHAT DISTINGUISHES MENTAL PRAYER FROM VOCAL PRAYER. MENTAL PRAYER CONSIDERED AS A REGULAR EXERCISE. FACILITY OF THIS EXERCISE

26. According to the definition accepted in all Catechisms, prayer is an act by which we elevate our souls to God, to render him our homage, expose to him our necessities, and ask him for graces.

27. Prayer is, according to St. Augustine, an act of humility and piety by which the soul lovingly turns towards God. *Oratio est conversio mentis in Deum per pium et humilem affectum.* It is, says again the same Father, every pious or affectionate movement towards God: *quicumque pius affectus in Deum.* It is, as the Fathers further say, an elevation of the soul to God; *ascensio mentis in Deum;* because to approach God is to be elevated, since nothing is above God.

28. This act may consist of a simple thought, a remembrance, a reflection, a consideration, an invocation, a desire, a promise, or a protestation. It is always implicitly an act of faith, of hope, and at least the beginning of an act of charity.

29. This act may be repeated, prolonged, and assume diverse forms; then prayer becomes a communication of the soul with God: she converses with God, or rather, she reflects and she humbles herself before him; she gives expression to her sentiments, desires, needs, gratitude, etc. It is what the Fathers call *sermocinatio, conversatio, colloquium cum Deo;* it is a divine audience.

30. Prayer, according to the doctrine of theology, is an act of the virtue of religion; when it turns into a habit, it becomes a virtue which depends equally on the virtue of religion: every prayer is in fact a homage of humility and submission which honors God; indeed, the object of the virtue of religion is no other than the honor and worship which we render to God.

31. A peculiarity of prayer is to honor God by the demand or expectation of some special favor; thus prayer is the homage of filial confidence; it is, at the same time, an act of love and depends on the virtue of charity. The fundamental ideas on the nature of prayer will likewise serve to make you understand better its necessity and facility.

32. Let us first of all show in what mental prayer essentially consists and what distinguishes it from vocal prayer. Mental prayer (or meditation) is, according to the most ordinary definition, that prayer which is made in the interior of the heart without being produced outwardly by any word. In mental prayer, says St. Gregory the Great, the desires are the words of the soul: *animarum verba, ipsa sunt desideria.* According to this distinction, mental prayer is said to abide by the language of the soul; vocal prayer borrows the language of the lips: *oratio mentalis est locutio mentis, sicut oratio vocalis est locutio vocis.*

33. To come to a clearer and more exact distinction between these two kinds of prayers, we shall not stop at etymological appearances, we shall sound their bottom and investigate the very essence of these two kinds of prayer. At first, do not imagine, from the meaning of the words which serve to designate both the one and the other, that the so-called vocal prayer employs only words uttered in a more or less elevated tone of voice. You can, and in fact, you do often say in a low voice long vocal prayers, such as the breviary and the rosary. You can even perform a kind of vocal prayer without uttering words; this happens when merely with the eyes and mind, you read a prayer from a manual of piety. In like manner, we may perform mental prayer in a loud voice, which happens when we express outwardly the sentiments we feel interiorly.

34. Thus, a prayer may preserve the nature and characteristics of vocal prayer, although you do not give utterance to a single articulated word. A prayer may also preserve the nature and qualities of mental prayer, although you express your thoughts and sentiments by articulated words, whether in a subdued or high tone of voice.

35. What then constitutes a vocal or a mental prayer? The prayer commonly called *mental* possesses one peculiarity; i.e., in this pious exercise, the soul communicates with God without the intermediary of a formula composed in advance. She produces acts which remain purely interior, or, if she judges it proper, she sometimes gives to these interior acts an exterior form in terms which then present themselves spontaneously to her. She remains in conversation or in pious communication with God, following with simplicity the indications of faith, the attractions of grace, the impulses of the heart, and the inspiration of the subject of meditation.

36. In *vocal* prayer, on the contrary, the soul addresses God by a kind of intermediary; she makes use of prepared formulas, which she knows by heart or reads in a book; she draws from them, as from a source, thoughts and sentiments which she makes her own, through which she converses with God. A great number of these formulas deserve all our veneration; some were composed by saints, and have been officially adopted by the Church; some form a portion of the deposit of revelation and have God himself for their Author.

37. Accordingly, these two kinds of prayer are excellent and necessary. The Church imposes long vocal prayers on her ministers and the exercise of mental prayer on religious.

38. This distinction well-established, let us now examine more closely in what mental prayer consists. To think of God or of supernatural truths, with at least a virtual intention of doing Him homage: behold the double element which underlies every mental prayer, if by analysis we retrench from it what is not indispensable. Thus to speak briefly, every *pious thought,* every *pious wish* is a mental prayer, a beginning of meditation.

39. We may sometimes think that vocal prayer is for beginners, and mental prayer for those who are more advanced; this is an error.

Mental prayer, considered in its constitutive element, reduced to its utmost simplicity of a *pious thought,* is the primary condition, the principle, soul, and life of every vocal prayer, even of every action, good and meritorious before God. Behold, how Suarez sums up this doctrine: "Mental prayer is perfect by the operation of the soul alone, it requires no exterior sign whatever: vocal prayer is perfect only by the voice or expression of speech, but it necessarily supposes an interior act, which constitutes its form and life; for in the same manner as an external act without the internal can neither be good nor bad, and, in consequence, not moral, so exterior prayer without the interior does not merit the name of prayer."

40. St. Francis de Sales gives the term *interior* word to this element of every prayer and meritorious act: "There are two species of words," says this saint, "the vocal and the interior. Now it is the vocal word which causes to be heard what the interior has first conceived; and, since prayer is but a conversation with God, it is certain that to do it without attention is something very displeasing to him; and when we do so, we are guilty of a great incivility, and thereby like unto parrots, that talk without knowing what they say."

41. When this interior word is entirely wanting, there is no longer any mental or vocal prayer nor act of supernatural life; what is still called prayer is but a simple movement of the tongue and lips, of which God complains in these terms: "*Populus iste ore suo et labiis suis glorificat me, cor autem ejus longe est a me;* this people draw near me with their mouth, and with their lips glorify me, but their heart is far from me." (Isaias XXIX, 13.)

42. When this interior word is existing, everything in our life may and does change into prayer; when it accompanies and enlivens our actions, it is called the active meditation, and all our actions become prayers; when it is permanent, it is called the spirit of prayer, or with St. Francis de Sales, *vital prayer,* and we accomplish the precept of the Lord: "*Oportet semper orare, et non deficere;* we ought always to pray, and not to faint." (Luke XVIII, 1.)

43. This first method of making mental prayer has the greatest analogy with the exercise of the presence of God, with the practice of

ejaculatory prayers, with the purity of intention, with the habitual conformity to God's holy will; it is an excellent preparation for the exercise properly called meditation, and at the same time one of the most precious fruits we may derive therefrom; for this reason we will on every occasion recommend this life of prayer which combines with the active life.

44. Do not exclude God from what you habitually say or do; keep for him in your mind and heart that place which he everywhere occupies as the principle and end of all created things; acknowledge his sovereign rights, his necessary action, and omnipresence; behold him in all and everywhere, frequently revert your thoughts to him, contemplate him, speak to him, offer yourself to him, and all the actions of your life, even the most common, will constitute a true prayer, your life will be an uninterrupted prayer.

45. Such has been the life of Mary and Joseph at Nazareth. Could you doubt that the life of the Holy Family was not a continual meditation? And nevertheless, this life was outwardly a life similar to that of other persons; they did not always meditate, they did not continually say vocal prayers, but they were always with Jesus, they labored with him, contemplated him, loved him! Behold what our life can and ought to be by faith, by the prayer of faith, and presence of God!

46. Let us hear again our good St. Francis de Sales: "By this is not meant that we are to pray day and night in order to praise God without interruption; but it is as much as saying that we ought always to praise God with our hearts and affections, having our intention, as much as possible, continually directed towards him, doing all things for his greater glory and honor."

47. Nothing then is easier, nothing ought to be more common than the habit of prayer; i.e. the habitual elevation of the soul towards God. If this habitual prayer were not possible and even easy, do you believe that our divine Savior, who knew human nature perfectly well, would have made it a commandment: *"Oportet semper orare, et non deficere;* we ought always to pray and not to faint?" (Luke XVIII, 1.) Do you believe that St. Paul, following the teaching of the divine Master, would have said to us: *"Sive ergo manducatis, sive bibitis, sive*

aliud quid facitis, omnia in gloriam Dei facite; therefore whether you eat or drink, or whatsoever else you do; do all things to the glory of God?" (I Cor. X, 31.) Would the same Apostle have added: *"Sine intermissione orate;* pray without ceasing?" (I Thess. V, 17.)

48. Several Fathers of the Church teach, however, that the precept of our Savior, *"you ought always to pray,"* and others of a like nature, have reference also to prayer properly so-called, and not merely to that purity of intention continually entertained and often renewed. They say that in these and similar passages of the Sacred Books, the word *"always"* is synonymous with *"often,"* i.e., whenever an occasion presents itself. Thus, we say of a man who has a passion for study, that he *always studies,* of a glutton, that he *always eats* or *drinks,* of an idler given to sleep, that he *always sleeps.* From this, they conclude that frequent prayer is of divine precept.

49. Indeed, the Christian life, like the bodily life, stands incessantly in need of being restored; this restoration is done by a twofold alimentation. The corporal life is kept up, renewed, and strengthened by respiration and food proper to its constitution; in like manner the Christian life is kept up and continually restored by the supernatural respiration, which is the continual prayer, whose nature and character we have just been describing, and by a nourishment, which includes prayer properly so-called and the sacraments.

50. The respiration which continues during work and sleep does not dispense with the necessity of hours of repose and relaxation, where our only occupation consists in breathing freely, and even, if possible, to breathe an air purer than that of our workshops and studies, and then to complete our restoration by another nourishment equally indispensable. In like manner, the continued prayer, in the form of a pure intention, does not dispense with the special exercise of prayer: prayer thus practiced constitutes, with the sacraments, the substantial nourishment from which the soul cannot abstain without dying of starvation. The most elevated form of this prayer is mental prayer, an intimate communication with God, a true intercourse, a prolonged visit during which the soul is entirely occupied with God.

51. You are tempted to interrupt me here: "There lies just the difficulty of mental prayer," you repeat with many others. "I know neither what to say nor what to do, nor how to pass the time of the visit in a proper manner; I am doomed to be kept waiting in distractions and sometimes in weariness till it is over." This is, in fact, the general objection.

52. If the exercise of mental prayer were as difficult as you think, do you believe that the holy Fathers and ascetic authors would have recommended it so earnestly and so generally? Do you believe that the Church would have prescribed it to all the religious? Do you believe that the founders of religious orders would have obliged their disciples to lose, in some way, a certain time each day which could have been more usefully employed in works of zeal, of education, of study, or in other works? From the very fact that the saints recommend it to all Christians, that the Church prescribes it to all the religious without distinction, to the unlearned as well as to those who have received a developed literary training, may we not infer that mental prayer must be an easy thing?

53. This exercise is looked upon as difficult, if not impossible, because often we have a wrong idea of it. Only recall to mind the acts constituting the elements of every mental prayer. We remark at first their simplicity: whenever the mind stops at a consideration of God, of his sanctity, and of his mercy; when the heart is seized with a salutary fear at the thought of hell; when the will resolves to avoid sin, because it leads to hell, the soul produces acts which constitute the elements of mental prayer, nay, which are mental prayer. How many perform mental prayer in this manner without knowing it, without even knowing what is understood by mental prayer!

54. Thus, as we have previously said, every pious act of your soul, of any one of its faculties: intellect, memory, imagination, heart, or will; good thoughts, religious recollections, salutary desires, holy intentions, pious acts of fear, confidence, invocation, repentance, good purpose, love, oblation, are elements of mental prayer, which is composed only of such elements, of such acts familiar to you, which

constitute, as it were, your daily bread, and which, on this account, must be easy and natural to you.

55. When your soul dwells on any of these acts, i.e. on this simple thought of God, you remain, by the very fact, in mental prayer; whenever you strengthen these acts anew, whenever you augment their number by reproducing and varying them, when you complete them, when you prolong them by reflection, you prolong at the same time your mental prayer. Whenever you deduce other acts from these first acts, or other considerations from these first considerations because they are contained in them, you continue the exercise of mental prayer.

56. How often have you not already made mental prayer in such a manner during five or ten minutes, without being aware of it, without even doubting about it? So true it is, that mental prayer is something simple and easy! It is so natural to the Christian soul, that there is not a child which, having as yet hardly received some religious ideas from the lips and heart of its mother, has not prayed thus on more than one occasion. For the child, mental prayer consists in its pious wishes and holy promises, in those artless prayers, suggested by its earthly mother, and addressed to its heavenly mother, the Blessed Virgin Mary.

57. For young men and people living in the world, mental prayer consists in the return to themselves, similar to that of the prodigal son, *in se reversus;* they compare what they are with what they were; they remember the day of a good confession, or of the first communion; at a friend's death, they think of what will follow this life, or of eternity; after a deception, they reflect on the mutability of terrestrial things, and detach themselves therefrom. One day, it is a misfortune, or a casual circumstance; another day, it is a reading, or a word which moved your most secret feelings, and plunged you into salutary reflections, your soul dwells on these reflections, these sentiments, and repeatedly returns to them. How often have you not thus experienced regrets, formed desires and resolutions, which constituted true prayer of the heart, a true mental prayer! If it were possible to gaze into the deepest recesses of souls, we should ascertain that if these

souls, according to the testimony of Tertullian, are naturally Christian, they are also spontaneously drawn to acts of mental prayer, unless they are entirely corrupted by vice or by a godless education.

58. When you endeavor, during fifteen or thirty minutes to produce these acts, i.e. these considerations of the mind, these affections of the heart, these resolutions of the will, as we have enumerated them (art. 54), you make a meditation of fifteen or thirty minutes. Do not, however, forget an important remark: mental prayer thus prolonged for fifteen or thirty minutes is not so much the soul's evoking the acts proper to mental prayer, as the soul's exerting herself to evoke such acts during this interval. The sincere desire of communicating with God, or the attention, sometimes actual, sometimes virtual, is all that is in your power; it is also the only condition necessary to constitute the state of mental prayer. What is beyond this depends on many circumstances, and especially on God's designs over you.

59. St. Augustine has exhibited this doctrine beautifully, and he comes back on it in several of his works: "If you wish not to give up praying, do not give up desiring; your continual desire is a continual prayer: *ipsum desiderium tuum oratio tua est; si non vis intermittere orare, noli intermittere desiderare; continuum desiderium tuum continua vox tua est.*" (St. Augustine.) Now what is easier, more natural, I will even say, more necessary to a poor and miserable soul, than to desire and then to ask for what is wanting to her, for what would relieve her, or contribute to her happiness?

60. Since mental prayer, according to the testimony and experience of the saints, is of all religious exercises that which offers the strongest guarantees to the soul for the assurance of her salvation, her advancement in virtue, and her final perseverance, is it astonishing that men who are possessed of convictions, that earnest Christians have made it a law for themselves regularly to perform mental prayer? Who would not be able to find a few minutes, a quarter of an hour during the day for this holy exercise? It is so much the easier as this short time reserved for mental prayer will be largely compensated by one of the fruits of this exercise, i.e. the good use of time.

61. On this account, the regular practice of mental prayer is prescribed by wise directors especially to those persons who find themselves inadequate for the occupations inherent to the duties of their state. They give two reasons for this: first, that this exercise is the only preservative against routine and dissipation, into which exterior affairs are likely to draw them; second, that mental prayer only can put them in a condition of properly regulating their time, by dividing it according to the importance of each affair. For these motives, St. Bernard recommended to Pope Eugenius III the frequent and daily exercise of mental prayer; and we may add that, if the pope had not followed this counsel of his master St. Bernard, we would not now invoke him as Blessed Eugenius III.

62. This is likewise the cause of the universal custom of placing the daily practice of mental prayer among the duties of the state of life professed by the religious, whatever be the importance and multiplicity of their functions. "It is a principle of the spiritual life, that without mental prayer, it is impossible for man to elevate himself to perfection. Mental prayer is the common source of all virtues; therefore the member of the Society of Mary endeavors principally to excel in this exercise; the more he devotes himself to it, the more he approaches his end." "Within the community or without, in whatever employment and circumstance a member may be, he makes an hour's meditation each day, ordinarily performed at two different times." "Every employment which would make it impossible for a Brother to perform mental prayer, is regarded as incompatible with the holiness of the state which he has embraced." (Constitutions S. M.)

63. The exercise of piety prescribed, under the name of meditation, to the religious of every order by their rules or by a custom which has become a law, is that of mental prayer, whose elements we have just been studying, which the masters of the spiritual life have all understood in the same manner, and which St. Francis de Sales defines in these terms: "Meditation is only an attentive thought, voluntarily repeated or nourished in our mind, in order to move the will to holy and wholesome affections."

64. Regular mental prayer, such as it is practiced in religious communities, is nevertheless distinguished by characteristics not belonging to mental prayer as practiced freely by each one individually; it is uniformly regulated for all the members of the community, by directions concerning the time, place, length, and frequency of this exercise, as well as certain details which refer to the method.

65. Considered as an exercise of the Rule, mental prayer, however, does not change either in its nature or in its form and end; it preserves its proper character, its facility, and excellence. It remains still a simple application of the soul to divine things, and pious thoughts still constitute its elements. If it is prolonged, it is still a true interview, an intimate communication with God; but it becomes in a higher degree the family circle which is formed regularly each day at a determined hour and for a specified time. At these august *rendez-vous*, the Father of this family grants each of his children the honor of a private audience, that they may talk familiarly with him, and also in order to manifest his paternal benevolence.

66. Taking into account the general directions of religious rules, and observing the proper nature, the essential parts, and principal elements of mental prayer as prescribed by the Rule, we can now give a detailed definition of it, which will be a program of what is still to be said in the sequel. The exercise of mental prayer as prescribed by the rule is a regular *audience* in which: I. God permits us to approach his supreme majesty *by faith* and to remain in his holy *presence*, that we may render him our homage, lay our petitions before him, and receive his lights and graces (*prayer of faith and presence of God*). 2. He reveals himself to us, by his communications, his doctrine and works: our intelligence thus learns, by a series of considerations, to know him better, and to know ourselves better, as well as our duties and end (*prayer of meditation*). 3. By manifesting himself to our intelligence, God acts necessarily on our heart and awakens in it those sentiments or affections which are as elevated as they are various, expressed by impulses of faith, hope, love, admiration, by remorses and regrets, by acts of humility and confidence, and, above all, by repeated invocations and earnest supplications (*prayer of*

supplication). 4. In fine, through the mind and heart, God acts on our will; he moves it towards good, and confirms it in the best resolutions: this cannot take place except by the union or conformity of our will with the holy Will of God, the only and universal standard of all that is good *(prayer of union or of conformity of our will with God's will).*

67. After these explanations, we clearly see that the object of mental prayer is to conduct us, whoever we may be, to our end. What is, in fact, the end of man, of the Christian and the religious? Is it not to know, love, and serve God, and thus obtain eternal life? Is it not what we learn and practice whenever we make mental prayer? Should this long enumeration still present to you, at first sight, mental prayer as a complicated exercise, do not stop at this first impression; experience will soon prove to you that no other exercise is more conformable to the nature, aspirations, and end of the Christian soul.

4

WHY MENTAL PRAYER TAKES THE FIRST RANK AMONG RELIGIOUS EXERCISES

68. The object of the Guide, as we love to repeat, is not only to point out to you the road and to lead you thereon, but also to show, whenever an occasion presents itself, the necessity, excellence, and advantages of mental prayer: for the more elevated your idea of mental prayer is, the more you love and esteem it, the greater will be the ardor and constancy with which you will apply yourself to this holy exercise.

69. While collecting what the saints have handed down to us on the art of mental prayer, we have, at every step, met with eloquent testimonials of their predilection for this holy exercise. Without interdicting ourselves later on to recall frequently to your mind their examples and fervent exhortations, we have gathered here some of their maxims and words, which could even serve you as excellent subjects of mixed mental prayer; they would thus produce a lasting impression on your soul, and contribute to make of you a man of meditation.

70. All the saints, without exception, have ranked mental prayer first among religious exercises. St. Charles Borromeo, in a synod, went so far as to forbid the admission to the ecclesiastical state of all those who were not versed in mental prayer, whatever knowledge

they might otherwise be possessed of. Such unanimity can be explained only by the fact that this preference for mental prayer is supported by incontestable motives. The saints most celebrated for the number and importance of works they accomplished were at the same time those who were distinguished for faithfully devoting a considerable portion of the day to mental prayer. St. Francis of Assisi and St. Bonaventure were always united to God by prayer and meditation; St. Thomas Aquinas acknowledged that if he knew anything he had learned it at the foot of the crucifix, and it was in meditation that St. Vincent de Paul found nourishment for his charity. When in the division of time, the saints found it impossible to suffice for all, they acted as in the division of an inadequate fortune: the spiritual exercises were the privileged creditors of the liquidation. What is due to the exercises of piety comes first; if there be a deficit, the reduction will bear on the time required for the other occupations.

71. St. Ignatius says: "The spiritual exercises (i.e. mental prayer, their essential element) are the best of anything we can conceive, feel, and understand in this world, whether for the progress of each individual, or for the fruits, helps, and spiritual advantages that can be derived therefrom." "Mental prayer," still says the same saint, "is the shortest road to perfection." It is, as we have already shown, the food, soul, and life of the other spiritual exercises, which in reality do exist, are kept up, and become profitable only by mental prayer, and in the measure of perfection we have attained therein.

72. "As the fish can live in water only, as it languishes and dies when deprived of this element, so the soul cannot live without prayer, and when prayer is wanting, the soul begins to pine away." (St. Augustine.) In this, as in other passages, where this term recurs, the word prayer has the signification of mental prayer, without which there cannot be any true vocal prayer.

73. St. Alphonsus Liguori especially understands it thus: "I cannot help," he says, "from feeling pained when I see that, while the Sacred Books and the works of the Fathers so frequently recommend the exercise of prayer, there are so few other books, so few preachers and confessors who treat this subject; or if they do treat of it, it is too

briefly, and as it were in passing. For myself, convinced as I am of the necessity of prayer, I say that all the books on religious subjects, all preachers in their sermons, all confessors in the tribunal of penance, should endeavor, above everything else, to inculcate in the minds of those who read or hear them, the necessity of praying always, never ceasing to admonish them of it, and repeating to them: Pray, pray, pray, and do not cease to pray; if you pray, you will certainly save your soul; if you do not pray, you will certainly be damned."

74. "Out of the absolute necessity binding on us to pray, springs the moral necessity of mental prayer. In fact, when we do not meditate, and are continually distracted by the multiplicity of temporal concerns, we hardly know our spiritual necessities, the dangers we incur regarding our salvation, the means we should employ to vanquish our temptations, or even this necessity of prayer, equally binding on all men. In such a state of blindness, we abandon the exercise of prayer, and no longer praying, we are unavoidably lost." (St. Alphonsus Liguori.)

75. Without prayer, no salvation; without meditation, no prayer; such is the reasoning of St. Alphonsus Liguori, and this illustrious doctor of prayer, fearing not to have been sufficiently clear, adds: "Without mental prayer it is impossible to live without sin, as Cardinal Bellarmine used to say. What concerns myself, someone may answer, I do not practice prayer, but I say many vocal prayers." "It ought to be known," remarks St. Augustine, "that to obtain the graces of which we stand in need, it suffices not to pray with the lips, we must also pray with the heart... Now vocal prayers are most frequently said with distraction, with the voice of the body and not with that of the heart, especially when these prayers are very numerous, and, besides, said by persons who do not practice mental prayer; on that account, God seldom listens to them, and rarely grants their request."

76. "Many persons," continues St. Alphonsus Liguori, "recite the rosary, the office of the Blessed Virgin, practice other exterior acts of piety, and still remain in mortal sin; but it is impossible that he who perseveringly makes mental prayer should remain in mortal sin:

either he will abandon meditation or he will abandon sin." St. Philip Neri, a great servant of God, was accustomed to say: "Mental prayer and sin cannot dwell together." Indeed, experience proves that those who give themselves to mental prayer do not fall so easily into disgrace with God; and if they should unhappily yield to mortal sin, they will re-enter into themselves and return to God, provided they only do not abandon meditation. "However relaxed a soul may be," says St. Teresa, "if she perseveres in mental prayer, the Lord will finally bring her to the port of salvation."

77. If sin and the spirit of prayer cannot remain together, it follows that a sinner, who makes meditation, is obliged to renounce, as it were, his unhappy condition. It must be added that the practice of meditation preserves us from many temptations and cautions us against those which we cannot avoid, so that they may give us an opportunity for victory and merit. "When the demons," says St. John Chrysostom, "perceive that we are armed with meditation, they take to flight as much precipitation as thieves who are caught and who already behold the sword lifted up over their heads." "There is nothing," resumes St. Philip Neri, "which the demon fears more than prayer, and nothing which he endeavors more to destroy in souls than the spirit of prayer." This is a commentary of these words of our Savior: "*Vigilate et orate ut non intretis in tentationem:* watch and pray, that ye enter not into temptation." (Matt. XXVI, 41.)

78. An evil more dangerous in its consequences than even a fall into sin, is lukewarmness. To deliver or preserve us from lukewarmness, we know of no more efficacious remedy than prayer: it is, so to say, the only remedy. The lukewarm man has lost all taste for spiritual things; he is blind, deaf, hardened, insensible to grace and to every supernatural solicitation. The most solemn truths are for him like a sealed book, or like a language he does not understand. What will enlighten his intellect, touch his heart, speak to his will, that his soul may shake off this deadly torpor? Mental prayer, mental prayer joined to vocal prayer.

79. It is to lukewarm souls especially that this declaration of St. Alphonsus Liguori ought to be repeatedly told: "He that prays will

certainly be saved, he that does not pray will certainly be damned."
All the saints have been saved by prayer, all the reprobate have been
damned for not praying. If the damned had prayed, they would
certainly not be lost. For this reason, their most agonizing subject of
despair in hell will be the thought that they might so easily have
saved themselves, by asking of God those graces of which they stood
in need, but which they can no longer do. Neglect of meditation is
one of the most certain signs of tepidity. Well does the devil know
what he is doing when he brings the soul to this fatal neglect, which
is both the cause and effect of tepidity.

80. "Perseverance in our vocation, success in the functions
imposed upon us, victory over temptations, return to God after the
commission of sin, lastly, final perseverance: should not all this be
considered as fruits produced solely by mental prayer?" (St. Vincent
de Paul.) Thus, through meditation, we are delivered from all evils,
and obtain all blessings. "In meditation, we possess a universal
weapon, and one most appropriate to all our necessities; it constitutes for each of us an undiminishing treasure, inexhaustible riches,
a port where all is in security, a place of calm and peace; it is the principle, the mother, the source, and root of all blessings." (St. Augustine.) "Meditation is the basis and foundation of solid virtues; if the
foundation begins to be defective, the building will soon fall." (St.
Teresa.)

81. "Nothing favors our progress in virtue more than to be with
God and to converse with him, which happens whenever we practice
mental prayer." (St. Augustine.) "He that is not a man of meditation
will never arrive at a high degree of sanctity, nor will he ever overcome himself. All that cowardice and immortification found in religious souls proceeds only from having neglected meditation, which is
the shortest and most efficacious means for the acquisition of
virtues." (St. Aloysius Gonzaga.)

82. Mental prayer does not only lead to the acquisition of virtue,
but it is itself the exercise of every virtue. "Mental prayer," says
Suarez, "includes all the interior acts, by which God may be
honored... it makes us practice, not merely one virtue, but all virtues."

"When the spirit of prayer takes possession of a soul, all the virtues enter therein at the same time." (St. Augustine.)

83. After this, is it necessary to add that meditation contributes most efficaciously to dispose God in our favor? God accords his choice graces only to men of meditation: "A religious ought principally to desire the spirit of mental prayer. I believe that without it we cannot obtain special graces from Almighty God." (St. Francis of Assisi.) St. Francis is himself a living proof of this truth. All historians unanimously say that mental prayer is the first source of all the wonders God was pleased to work in the person and through the medium of this humble servant. Hence from the day of his conversion, he was so faithful in this holy exercise that in health as in sickness, he devoted the greater part of the day to it. Before undertaking anything, he consulted God and gathered strength in meditation; at home as well as abroad, in going about, at work or at rest, his spirit was in heaven, he was conversing with God in meditation.

84. Our perfection consists in our resemblance to God; the greater our conformity with God, the more holy and perfect is our soul. Mental prayer renders this wonderful transformation of the soul possible; for as iron is made supple by fire, and fit to receive the form which we wish it to retain afterwards, in like manner does meditation dispose the soul to receive, under the influence of grace, those features and virtues, which, day after day, complete her resemblance to God, to such a degree, that she beholds all things in the light of God, appreciates them, speaks of them, loves or rejects them as God does; her desires and inclinations are like those of God; she acts and lives in God, with him and for him. "The colocynth," says St. Francis de Sales, "never tastes so bitter, than when we have eaten honey. When we shall have tasted divine things, the pleasures of this world will no longer give us any relish." "Children learn to speak the language of their mothers," adds the same Saint, "by hearing them speak and lisping with them; and we, dwelling near our Savior in mental prayer, by observing his words, actions, and affections, shall, with the help of his grace, learn to speak, act, and wish as he does."

85. To sum up, when mental prayer is lacking, nothing can supply

this defect; on the contrary, when all the means of salvation and perfection are taken from us, mental prayer supplies them all. The solitaries of the desert had neither exhortations, nor community exercises, nor even Holy Communion, except at rare intervals; but they had the habitual practice of mental prayer, and this sufficed to raise them to sublime sanctity.

86. Should even meditation be neither advantageous nor necessary, we ought still to practice it with the greatest eagerness: Is it not a supreme honor for us? "Who would not be struck with astonishment and admiration, considering the goodness of God towards us, the incomparable honor he confers on us in judging us worthy of conversing with him, and of offering him our wishes?" (St. Augustine.) Is it not already an astonishing prodigy, that man, who is nothing but dust and ashes, be admitted to a divine audience? And yet, this is not all, for God has deigned to invite us, to press us, to await us, and make us the most magnificent promises, as if he were to be benefited by this ineffable condescension. "This honor," adds St. Augustine, "surpasses the dignity of the angels; it is so sublime that our reason is unable to comprehend it in all its grandeur."

87. Can we not share in the enthusiasm of St. Augustine, repeating with him: "*Quid est oratione præclarius? Quid vita nostræ utilius? Quid animo dulcius? Quid in tota nostra religione sublimius?* Is there anything more honorable, more useful to our life, more delicious to our soul, more sublime in our holy religion than mental prayer?" "Therefore it is an evident sign of folly not to understand the greatness of the honor there is in prayer, and not to love this holy exercise." (St. John Chrysostom.) Has not this been our folly for too long a time? How many hours, how many graces we have lost! In order to guard against such losses during the remainder of our life, let us not pass a day without having examined ourselves on our fidelity in the exercise of mental prayer.

5

HOW WE ARE TO MAKE MENTAL PRAYER, AND FIRST, HOW WE ARE TO DISPOSE OURSELVES FOR IT IN OUR DAILY LIFE BY THE "REMOTE PREPARATION"

88. After these preliminary notions, we finally come to the exercise of mental prayer itself. It is, as we have said, a *divine audience.* We shall frequently revert to this comparison; it will help us better to understand, retain, and classify our counsels and explanations.

89. In every audience deserving of this name, certain things are to be done and observed: 1. *previous* to the audience, to prepare worthily for it; 2. *during* the audience, to employ the time properly; 3. *after* the audience, to bring it to a successful termination. This gives us the three parts of mental prayer; you know the names by which they are generally designated: 1. the *preparation;* 2. the *body* of *mental prayer;* 3. the *conclusion.*

90. Any person who obtains an audience of the Pope or the Sovereign, esteems himself happy on account of this mark of honor and benevolence; he cannot help thinking of it; he prepares and foresees whatever could dispose the Pope or Sovereign in his favor. Are you not the object of a distinction a thousand times more desirable? Are you not invited to a far more august audience? Could you allege any excuse if, in your levity and indifference, you would go so far, as not even to judge it worthy of previous consideration?

91. Faith and reason both make known to the Christian and even

impose on him the duties which prepare him to appear before God in a worthy manner. Of these duties, we shall mention the principal ones, from which the others are derived. They are, besides a great esteem of this favor, separation from whatever could displease the Divine Majesty, and the research for whatever could merit us a favorable reception.

92. "Si *scires donum Dei,* if thou didst know the gift of God!" (St. John IV, 10.) It is truly the case to repeat this word here, for never shall we be able to understand fully the honor God does us in calling us to a confidential audience which is a true and most cordial tête-à-tête. Never cease, even after twenty or forty years of practice, to question your faith on the mystery of mental prayer, because it will unfold to your view, each day, new subjects of admiration; never will you understand the Supreme Being of God, your nothingness, and, in consequence, what ought to be the nature of the interview between the Creator and the creature, between such a Father and such a child! *Da mihi intellectum* (Ps. CXVIII.), Lord, give me understanding of these things, and do not permit that I ever regard them with indifference.

93. The principal obstacles which prevent us from making mental prayer well are attachment to sin, slavery of the senses and passions, especially dissipation, and immortification of the tongue.

94. In proportion as faith will enlighten you more vividly about the majesty of God, and the baseness of your nonentity, you will feel impelled, when on the point of being admitted into the presence of God, to remove whatever could be offensive in his sight, and in the first place, to remove sin. Our Lord has declared: "Blessed are the clean of heart, for they shall see God." Without purity of heart, we cannot be allowed to see God, to present ourselves before him, to speak to him as it is done in mental prayer, because sin constitutes a wall of separation between God and man.

95. But remark it well; it is properly the malice of sin, i.e. the inordinate will, which constitutes this obstacle; remove obstinacy, guilty complacency in sin, and the wall of separation will crumble, and with the prodigal son, the penitent Magdalen, the Samaritan woman, the

good thief, you will obtain a hearing, and like the publican, you will return filled with benedictions. Who could hinder the sinner from drawing near to God? Perhaps our Lord? But remember what he said: "I came to call the sinners, and not the just: those that are sick stand in need of physician." Therefore, neither past nor actual sins are an obstacle; on the contrary, they establish a more urgent necessity to go to God, and even present a greater facility of being eagerly received. The Gospel confirms it; try, sinners.

96. Falls and relapses into sin, when they are the result of our weak nature and inconstant will, bad habits which we endeavor to overcome, are precisely cured by the exercise of mental prayer; but the voluntary attachment to sin, however much it may be concealed by exterior practices of piety, great activity, continual labor, and even by the tears and sighs of tenderness; also affection for certain favorite sins, though otherwise not very grievous in themselves: behold what hinders us when we present ourselves before God to converse with him in mental prayer.

97. We have also mentioned the slavery of the senses and passions which keep us under the shameful yoke of the devil: he who habitually seeks his gratification in eating and other gross enjoyments will never be a man of meditation. "The sensual man," says St. Paul, "perceiveth not the things that are of the Spirit of God. *Animalis homo non percipit ea quæ sunt Spiritus Dei.*" (I Cor. II, 14). It is superfluous to insist on this point, for who does not understand that there can be no more intimate relation between God and the man who is a slave of Satan, than there can be between light and darkness, between day and night? When one comes, the other disappears.

98. An obstacle to every serious intercourse with men and *a fortiori* with God is the want of restraint in speech, a habitual dissipation, which results from lack of control over one's self, over the mind and heart, and which never leaves man the possibility to state with any certainty, at any moment, what he will say or do the next moment. Hence he who is conscious of being subject to this fault should incessantly struggle against it, till it be overcome; otherwise, he will never be a man of mental prayer. Recollection, a habit of

silence, is an indispensable condition of success in mental prayer: "*Ducam eam in solitudinem, et loquar ad cor ejus.* I will allure her, and will lead her into the wilderness: and I will speak to her heart." (Osee II, 14) Before God speaks to a soul, she must be in the solitude of recollection. Further on, we shall have occasion to indicate the manner of combating dissipation.

99. All that keeps us from God, and repels us when endeavoring to approach him, is summed up in pride, in the search of our own gratification, in one word, in the more or less avowed worship of ourselves. In order to find God, we must, after all, deny ourselves; hence, the necessity of renunciation, self-denial, mortification, and all the other virtues which are death to the old man; hence, also, the necessity of humility which alone can introduce us to God, and draw down upon us the regards of his benevolence and the effusion of his graces. To a person who asked how to make meditation, St. Philip Neri answered: "Be humble and obedient and the Holy Spirit will teach you what you desire to know." And in another place: "An excellent means to learn how to make mental prayer is to consider oneself unworthy of this benefit."

100. "The true preparation for mental prayer consists in mortification; he who wishes to make meditation without mortifying himself, is like a bird that attempts to fly before it has feathers." (St. Philip Neri.) St. Vincent de Paul says: "The best disposition we can bring to prayer and meditation is humility, the conviction of our nothingness, the mortification of our passions and natural inclinations, which entice us into sin, interior recollection, purity of intention, remembrance of God's presence, entire conformity to his will, frequent aspirations to his divine Goodness."

101. The habitual remembrance of God, kept up by frequent aspirations, is a remedy against dissipation, favors interior recollection, and leads us to dispose our soul in such a manner as to render her pleasing to God. On this account, the masters of the spiritual life recommend these practices with as much strength as unanimity. "In the exercises of the spiritual retreat (i.e. spiritual recollection) and ejaculatory prayers," says St. Francis de Sales, "lies the greatness of

devotion. It supplies the want of all other prayers; but its absence can scarcely ever be filled in any other way."

102. "It is admitted as a principle that he who does not adopt the happy custom of living in God's presence, will never be a man of meditation. We strangely deceive ourselves in believing that it suffices to make, by routine, some acts of faith, adoration, humility, contrition, before entering upon the subject-matter of meditation. These acts, said in a purely mechanical way, signify nothing, do not, in the least, make the soul recollected, but leave her open to distractions and dissipation." (Father Chaminade.)

103. "Nothing," continues St. Francis de Sales, "nothing so well disposes the soul to an intimate union with God than the frequent use of ejaculatory prayers." Let us take care to begin no action without offering it to the Lord; and, whatever be our occupation, let us not even spend one quarter of an hour without raising our hearts to God by a fervent act of piety. Let us also endeavor to profit, as much as possible, from every leisure moment to unite ourselves to God; as when we are expecting someone, or when going from one place to another, or when confined to bed by sickness.

6

HOW WE MUST PREPARE OURSELVES FOR MENTAL PRAYER DURING THOSE MOMENTS THAT PRECEDE THE EXERCISE, OR HOW TO MAKE THE "PROXIMATE PREPARATION"

104. When the time for meditation approaches, ponder over the subject of the audience, and make your final arrangements. To think of nothing would be exposing oneself to appear before God like a man who knows neither what to say nor what to do, i.e. like a man who tempts God. "*Ante orationem præpara animam tuam, et noli esse quasi homo qui tentat Deum.*" (Ecclesiasticus XVIII, 23). Here again, faith and the simplest notions of propriety require, besides greater recollection at the approach of meditation: 1) the selection of the subject; 2) exactness for the hour and place of rendezvous.

105. The selection of the subject bears relation to the fruit or result you wish to derive from this intercourse. It is made in the evening for the meditation of the next morning; for the evening meditation it is done in the course of the day, for instance, during a visit to the Most Holy Sacrament, or during spiritual reading: what it imports you is that you have a fixed time for making this choice. Sometimes you may abide by the subject chosen for the entire community and read by the religious charged with this duty; sometimes you may foresee a particular subject, relating to the state of your soul; sometimes you may revert to a subject already known and meditated upon, revolving it rapidly in your mind; lastly, you may,

from time to time, meditate upon a text taken from a good book you have with you. In all this, you will be guided by the end you propose to yourself, and which is no other than the fruit of the meditation. It happens sometimes also that God chooses the subject for you, either by speaking to your heart or striking your mind by the remembrance of a past event, by an unforeseen issue, or by a sudden spectacle. When God speaks to us first, it is our duty to listen and to follow; but he did not bind himself to furnish us with a subject for the interview; we are therefore obliged to select it ourselves.

106. According to these principles, those souls given to trouble and to fear will meditate oftener on the goodness and mercy of God, on the beautiful and touching parables of the Gospel relating to this subject, on the Holy Eucharist, and more frequently on the Passion of Jesus Christ. It seems to us that a true disciple of our Lord, whatever the state of his soul may be, ought to meditate on the Passion at least once a week.

107. The great truths of our religion, the last things of man, sin, tepidity, etc., will also furnish useful subjects of meditation each week, except for timorous souls, such as we have just mentioned. Prayer, in general, considered as the great means of salvation, the principal prayers and ordinary practices of the Christian, morning and evening prayers, holy Mass, confession, communion, practices of piety to the Sacred Heart, to the Blessed Virgin, and other fundamental devotions: behold another source of subjects from which we should not fail to draw frequently. Finally, the Gospel, the life and teachings of our Divine Master, evidently constitute the most abundant source.

108. In the choice of subjects, we would do well to adapt them to the feasts which the Church celebrates and to the mysteries which she commemorates on certain days and at certain periods. Thus, during Advent and after Christmas, we may meditate sometimes on the incarnation and Childhood of our Savior; during Lent, on the Passion; during Easter time, on his Resurrection, etc.; Thursdays, on the Most Holy Sacrament; Fridays, on our Lord's Passion; and Saturdays, on the Blessed Virgin.

109. All these subjects are treated in meditation books; these books are a great help, but only on condition that we do not take the subjects in the order of succession day after day. No book could have its contents so disposed as to be best suited each day to the wants of a community or an individual. The wants and state of a soul depend on many circumstances which make it impossible to foresee a long time in advance. Often it happens that the appropriateness of a meditation strikes us more than the subject itself; therefore, we repeat, as to what regards the subject of meditation, let us not regret the time we spend in making a good choice of it.

110. We say that this choice depends greatly on the dispositions of those who make meditation. The masters of the spiritual life do, indeed, distinguish three states in the Christian life: the state of those who commence, the state of those who advance, and the state of those who have reached the end; in other words, the beginners, the intermediate, and the perfect. It suffices to indicate this distinction that you may at once perceive it to be founded on reason. It is not established according to the intensity of the dispositions, but according to the nature of the acts and efforts proper to each class; if it were founded on their intensity, really, the number of distinctions and degrees would be almost infinite.

111. The beginners are evidently those that put themselves to the work, and are determined to serve God according to their duty. Their principal labor is to put to death the old man, by waging war against sin, and especially against the habit of sin. For them, the subjects of meditation turn most frequently on the solemn truths of our holy religion: the end of man, salvation, sin and its ravages in the soul, its punishment and expiation in the fallen angels, in our first parents, in the Passion and Death of our Lord; the four last things: death, judgment, hell, and heaven. To these subjects we may add others capable of reanimating hope and love; like the parable of the prodigal Son, of the good Shepherd, and the kindness of Jesus in receiving penitent sinners. They should also meditate on Mary's tender love and compassion for contrite sinners, whose assured refuge she is, etc. Thus, the beginners endeavor to awaken in their hearts sentiments of

repentance, confusion, and fear, afterwards of confidence and love; but above all, they take a firm resolution, cost what it may, to fight against sin and whatever leads to it. This state of things will last as long as the passions are not easily overcome, and mortal sins not habitually avoided.

112. The intermediate, or those who advance, are such Christians as try to put on Jesus Christ by the imitation of his virtues; they succeed in avoiding mortal sins habitually, but easily fall into venial sins, allow themselves to be drawn to exterior things, and are not sufficiently master over the movements of their hearts. They, however, understand the excellence of the Christian life, the beauty of virtue. They endeavor not to commit venial sins deliberately and purposely. The most appropriate subjects of meditation for them are the examples of our Lord, of the most Blessed Virgin, and the Saints, also the advantages arising from the practice of virtue. It is likewise useful for them to take as subjects of meditation, the commandments of God and the Church, the duties of their state, etc.; and if they are religious, the Rule and evangelical counsels, the Christian and religious virtues, such as faith, hope, charity, humility, self-denial, poverty, chastity, obedience, prudence, justice, fortitude, temperance, etc.

113. Those who find their greatest happiness in the remembrance and service of God are called the perfect; they abhor venial as well as mortal sins. They are habitually united with Him by the thought of His presence, the purity of their intention, their conformity to His holy Will, i.e. by the bonds of a perfect love. They meditate with ease and profit on God and His attributes, chiefly on His goodness and mercy, on His love for man, on the mysteries of our holy religion, the Holy Eucharist, the Passion, etc.

114. These three states are also called the purgative, the illuminative, and the unitive way; or also, the state of penitence, of justice, and of perfection; everyone will easily understand the reasons for these denominations. Remark it well, however, that this distinction cannot be absolute. In fact, perfection, in this world, has its shortcomings and imperfections, and many a sinner is capable of generous efforts

without quitting the state of beginners. We find ourselves in one or the other of these three states, according as the characters of that state predominate in us. It is scarcely necessary to say that the duration of these states is not the same for all.

115. We have said that mental prayer is a divine audience. We should be inexcusable, were we to miss the time appointed for an audience with which a great personage would honor us; ought we to have less regard for Almighty God than for an earthly prince? Arrange therefore your affairs so as to cause neither delay nor omission; the hour of the Rule is God's hour: never forget it, if you wish to become a man of meditation.

116. In all religious orders, mental prayer takes place in the first morning hour, and when it is divided into two parts, the second part takes place in the evening. "*Mane et vespere tempus est orationis opportunum.*" (St. Bonaventure.) Reason and faith are in accordance on this point. For it is in the morning that the children gather around their father to receive his orders, advices, counsels, encouragements, and blessing for the daily labors. "*Cor susum tradet ad vigilandum diluculo ad Dominum qui fecit ilium, et in conspectu Altissimi deprecabitur.* The wise man will give his heart to resort early to the Lord, that made him: and he will pray in the sight of the most High." (Eccl. XXXIX, 6.) "*Oportet prævenire solem ad benedictionem tuam, et ad ortum lucis te adorare.* We ought to prevent the sun to bless thee, and adore thee at the dawning of the light." (Wisdom XVI, 28.) "*In matutinis meditabor in te:* I will meditate on thee in the morning" (Ps. LXIII, 7.), lastly says the Royal Prophet. In the evening the children feel happy to reassemble for a few moments around their father, to give him an account of their day's work, humbly to avow their negligences and ask his pardon, to tell him how happy they are in serving such a father and also to receive a last blessing before lying down to sleep. The Divine Master himself was accustomed to retire in the evening into solitude for prayer. "The body should not lie down to rest before the soul has been strengthened by meditation, which is its food. *Non prius corpusculum requiescat quam anima pascatur.*" (St. Jerome.) A recollection or a meditation of a few minutes at this time of the day is never impossi-

ble, whatever be the circle in which we move or the press of business incumbent on us.

117. "He that seeks God, finds him everywhere and at all times," says St. Alphonsus Liguori; we can therefore meditate, as we have already said, in any place, at home and elsewhere, even while walking, working, or traveling. But when there is question of an exercise of the Rule, God awaits us where the community assembles. Special graces are attached to prayers said in common: "*Ubi enim sunt duo vel tres congregati in nomine meo, ibi sum in medio eorum,* For where there are two or three gathered together in my name, says our Lord, there am I in the midst of them." (Matt. XVIII, 20.) He that fails to be present at the rendez-vous, will deprive himself of those special graces. If anyone should, however, be kept away from the community, not by any fault of his own, but on account of his duties, he would share in all the advantages of his fellow-brothers. What can be wanting to us, when we are where God wishes us to be? Does he not await us there where he calls us?

118. If you are sometimes obliged to make meditation in a place which does not seem proper, recall to mind the examples of the saints, who knew how to be recollected and to pray in the midst of tumult when they were prevented from retiring into privacy. St. Catherine of Siena was accustomed to consider her body as a temple. When St. Philip Neri was walking through the streets, he was so bereft of his senses, that he stood in need of a monitor who would warn him to salute those who had a right to this mark of attention.

119. Undoubtedly, the indispensable condition is the solitude of the heart; but the solitude of the body is also required. Our Savior himself recommends it: "*Tu autem, cum oraveris intra in cubiculum tuum, et clauso ostio, ora Patrem tuum in abscondito.* When thou shalt pray, enter into thy chamber, and having shut the door, pray to thy Father in secret." (Matt. VI, 6.) Let us then look for tranquility as much as we can, although by itself it would not suffice: "*Quid prodest solitudo corporis, si solitudo defuerit cordis?*" (St. Gregory Nazianzen.)

120. But the proper place for prayer, according to the testimony of our Lord himself, is the church, the chapel, the oratory: first, because

it is the house of God, *domus Patris mei* (St. John II, 16.); is it not meet that we visit God where he deigns to reside? Then, because the church is a house of prayer, the house which God has given us as our rendez-vous: *Domus mea, domus orationis est.* (Luke XIX, 46.): Finally, it is in a particular manner proper to make the meditation before the Holy Tabernacle. *Ecce tabernaculum Dei cum hominibus;* there it is that God meets man. On this account our Rules invite us to make our meditation at this place whenever it is possible.

WHAT IS TO BE DONE AT THE BEGINNING OF MENTAL PRAYER, OR IN WHAT THE "IMMEDIATE PREPARATION," OR THE "PRAYER OF FAITH" AND OF THE "PRESENCE OF GOD" CONSISTS

121. By the immediate preparation, we are, in some manner, ushered into the divine presence; this preparation is done at the very hour and place of rendezvous with God, and comprises: i) the invocation of the Holy Ghost, the Blessed Virgin, and our guardian angel who acts as usher; ii) an act of faith in God's presence, and of union with our Lord; iii) other acts which follow from this act of faith; as, acts of humility, confidence, adoration, etc. During these acts or at their close, we proceed to the subject of the interview.

122. The invocation of the Holy Ghost and the Blessed Virgin, for which we make use of the well-known formula, the *Veni Sancte* and *Ave Maria,* is placed at the commencement of our principal actions. Mental prayer is a supernatural act for which the cooperation of the Holy Spirit is directly necessary: because as stated in the definition, all the acts of mental prayer are produced under the influence of grace. We must therefore apply unreservedly to prayer, what our Lord and the Apostles teach us about our utter impossibility of producing by ourselves, i.e. without supernatural help, the least act of this nature. "*Sine me nihil potestis facere;* without me you can do nothing." (St. John XV, 5.) "*Non sumus sufficientes cogitare aliquid ex nobis quasi ex*

nobis; sed sufficientia nostra ex Deo est. Not that we are sufficient to think anything of ourselves, as of ourselves: but our sufficiency is from God." (2 Cor. III, 5.) "*Nemo potest dicere, Dominus Jesus nisi in Spiritu Sancto.* And no man can say, the Lord Jesus, but by the Holy Ghost." (1 Cor. XII, 3.) How often do we not spend the time of meditation without doing anything, because we rely too much on ourselves, because we neglect to invoke the Holy Spirit, and do not continue to invoke him till he deigns to pray in us and by us.

123. The Holy Spirit who dwells in us comes to our assistance by making us understand our misery clearly, as well as our impossibility of quitting that state. 2. By uniting his strength to our weakness, his light to our ignorance, he helps us know what is useful to us. 3. By joining his own voice, his own demand, and his unspeakable groanings to our voice: "*Spiritus adjuvat infirmitatem nostram; nam quid oremus sicut oportet, nescimus; sed ipse Spiritus postulat pro nobis gemitibus inenarrabilibus.* The Spirit also helpeth our infirmity; for we know not what we should pray for as we ought: but the Spirit himself asketh for us with unspeakable groanings." (Rom. VIII, 26.) Later on, we shall speak of the particular motives we have to invoke the most blessed Virgin at the beginning of meditation.

124. Then follows the act of faith in the presence and mission of our guardian angel. By God's will, he is our official usher, for it is his office to present our prayers to God. "*Ascendit fumus incensorum de orationibus sanctorum de manu Angeli coram Deo:* the smoke of the incense of the prayers of the saints ascended up before God, from the hand of the angel." (Apoc. VIII, 4.) It is fitting to add analogous acts of faith and of invocation to the guardian angels of the sanctuary, if the meditation is made before the blessed Sacrament; to your holy Patrons, to the saints whose feast is celebrated, and especially to St. Joseph, who is, by excellence, the man of meditation. Could we ever extend too far our care of being well surrounded, when about to appear before the immortal King of angels and saints? "St. Augustine relates that when he was still a Manichean, he one day entered a church, where St. Ambrose had the office chanted alternately in two

choirs, as it is still done nowadays: at which he was so enraptured and beside himself in beholding the beautiful order and reverence preserved thereat, that he thought himself in paradise: and many saints affirm that they have often seen angels coming in great numbers to assist at the divine offices. With what attention and reverence ought we to assist at them, since the angels are there present and repeat on high, in the triumphant Church, what we are saying here below in the militant Church!" (St. Francis de Sales.)

125. The introduction, properly so-called, consists in an act of faith in the presence of God; it is the most important act of the immediate preparation. It is never to be omitted; for, by it, we place ourselves in the sight of God, which is the condition strictly required for succeeding in the interior acts. *"Credere enim oportet aecedentem ad Deum, quia est:* for he that cometh to God, must believe that he is" (Hebr. XI, 6.), which implies his presence.

126. Do not imagine that this act is difficult, that it requires a kind of ecstasy which would transport you to the third heaven, or the vigorous effort of a powerful imagination, because you would then have a ready excuse in saying that you are neither a St. Paul, nor the possessor of fertile imagination. It is simply required to fix, by an act of faith, the eye of your soul on God, just as, by an act of your will, you direct the eye of your body towards any object you wish to contemplate. You have neither to go out of yourself nor to create illusions in your mind by imaginary suppositions: remain in the reality. Is God then so far from each one of us? Is it not in him that we live, move, and are? *"In ipso enim vivimus, et movemur, et sumus."* (Acts XVII, 28.) God is everywhere; he is more intimately present to us than our soul is to our body.

127. Generally, we are not even aware of the presence of God in and amongst us; hence we do not think of it. Thanks to our Lord Jesus Christ, this presence has become so intimate that it could not be more so. To give us an idea of it, our sacred books have recourse to the most striking images: Jesus Christ is our garment; his grace and merits cover and transform us in such a manner as to communicate

his likeness to us and change us into him. Jesus Christ is the vine, and we are the branches; we form but one with him, and from him we receive life, light, strength, and activity. The entire Church, composed of angels and men, does not form a family only, but a mystical body, which is the very Body of our Lord. Jesus Christ is the chief or head of this body; we are its members, and these members are more closely united with their Chief than the members of our body with its head, for the supernatural life is more perfect than the natural. Jesus Christ himself declares it; he is and desires to be in us; he wishes that we be in him, as he is in his Father. Find elsewhere a more intimate, more complete presence or penetration between two persons.

128. Listen to St. Augustine applying this doctrine to prayer: "God cannot make a more magnificent present to men than by constituting as their Chief his Word, through whom he created everything, and by uniting them to this Chief as true members of the same body, so that the Eternal Word is, at the same time, the Son of God and the Son of man, one God with his Father, one man with men. In consequence, whenever we speak to God in prayer, it is not done without the Son; when the body speaks, it is not without the Head: *Ut et quando loquimur ad Deum deprecantes, non inde Filium separemus; et quando precatur corpus Filii, non a se separet caput suum.* Thus the same Lord Jesus Christ, Savior of his own Body, prays, at the same time, for us, in us, and we pray to him: *Sitque ipse unus salvator corporis sui Dominus noster Jesus Christus Filius Dei, qui et oret pro nobis, et oret in nobis, et oretur a nobis.* He prays for us as our High-priest, he prays in us as our Head, we pray to him as to our God: *Orat pro nobis, ut sacerdos noster; orat in nobis, ut caput nostrum; oratur a nobis, ut Deus noster.* Then let us not fail to recognize, at the same time, our voice in him, and his voice in us. *Agnoscamus ergo et in illo vo-ces nostras, et voces ejus in nobis.* As God, he receives our prayers; as servant, he prays himself; there he is Creator, here he is created, and, without changing himself, he changes us into him, by making of us with him, i.e. of the body with the Head, but one man. *Oratur ergo in forma Dei, orat in forma servi; ibi Creator, hic creatus, creaturam mutandam non mutatus assumens, et secum nos faciens unum hominem, caput et corpus.* Therefore we pray to

him, we pray through him, and in him; the mental prayer, in which we are engaged, we make with him, and he with us; we make it in him and he in us. *Oramus ergo ad illum, per illum, in illo: et dicimus cum illo, et dicit nobiscum; dicimus in illo, dicit in nobis orationem. (Instr. LXXXV. Psalm.)*

129. Rev. Father Olier loved to recall frequently to the minds of his disciples this same doctrine — viz., Our Savior's presence in our souls, in order to make with us all the acts of the supernatural life: "Our Lord bestows himself unto us, he embalms our souls, and fills them with the interior dispositions of his religious spirit, so that of our souls and his, he makes but one, which he animates with the same spirit of respect, love, praise, and sacrifice... Our Lord desires that, by the operation of the Spirit, we should live in him a life truly one, as the Father and the Son live in each other, having but one life, one feeling, one desire, one love, as they are but one God living in two Divine Persons."

130. Is there a prayer more excellent, more efficacious, more meritorious, in a word, more Christian, than the prayer of Jesus Christ, our Head, speaking for and through his members, or the prayers of the members speaking through their Head? Is it not, in the highest degree, the prayer made in the name of the Lord? And does not the reproach addressed by the Divine Master to his Apostles signify, in its most elevated sense, that we do not think in our prayers of this union of the Head and members in the same body? "Hitherto you have not asked anything in my name. Ask, and you shall receive; that your joy may be full. *Usque modo non petistis quidquam in nomine meo; petite et accipietis,* ut *gaudium vestrum sit plenum.*" (St. John XVI, 24.)

131. What is wanting to us is not the presence of God, but the attention to this presence. Direct your attention to this truth to contemplate it in its splendor and extent; see how much the intimate reality differs from the outward appearance; make an act of faith in this fruitful reality: renew this act of faith by repeating the word *Credo,* and asking yourself: Have I had faith until this day? Do I believe at present? God is before me, he is within me? I am before God and in God? All the rest is as if it did not exist?

132. Remember some texts of our Sacred Books: "*Numquid non cœlum et terram ego impleo:* do I not fill heaven and earth?" (Jerem. XXIII, 24.) "*Medius vestrum stetit quem vos nescitis:* there hath stood one in the midst of you, whom you know not." (St. John I, 26.) "*Si ascendero in cœlum, tu illic es; si descendero in infernum, ades:* if I ascend into heaven, thou art there? If I descend into hell, thou art present." (Psalm CXXXVIII, 8.) "*Vivit Dominus, in cujus conspectu sto:* the Lord liveth, in whose sight I stand." (III Kings XVII, I.) "*Nescitis quia templum Dei estis, et Spiritus Dei habitat in vobis?* Know you not that you are the temple of God, and that the Spirit of God dwelleth in you?" (I Cor. III, 16.)

133. Love to repeat these and similar texts: add thereto these reflections: Do I believe this? Am I at present convinced of it? "I do believe, Lord; help thou my unbelief. *Credo, Domine, adjuva incredulitatem meam.*" (Mark IX, 23.) If we had only a little faith, the presence of God would occupy our minds more vividly than all creatures united could do. God the Father, while contemplating Jesus Christ, let this cry of his heart escape him: "This is my beloved Son, in whom I am well pleased; hear ye him." And we could remain insensible in the presence of him who fills the Heavenly Father with admiration! And we could remain cold, indifferent, when we are permitted to listen to him, to hear him speak! I ask you, where is our faith?

134. The habit of walking in the holy presence of God, out of the time of meditation, and the act of faith in this presence, at the commencement of meditation, are the most efficacious means to establish us in pious communication with God. For every interview, there must at least be two: when it is a question of the heavenly conversation called mental prayer, God is always ready; and all would go on wondrously well, if it could be added that we also are always ready. On account of the want of preparation, there are so few men of meditation: and what paralyzes our feeble efforts, even in the very preparation, is the lack of faith, the neglect of the acts of faith in the presence and other attributes of God.

135. This act of faith in the presence of God is not always made in the same manner; it should vary according to the state of your soul

and the immediate object of the audience, but always without being obliged to resort to imaginary suppositions. God is our *all,* according to the expression of St. Francis of Assisi and several other saints; therefore, we can represent him to ourselves under a thousand different aspects, and thus you possess the facility of varying almost indefinitely your act of faith in the presence of God.

136. According to circumstances, you may consider yourself before God as mere nothing, as a grain of sand in comparison with the Supreme Being, the Creator of heaven and earth; as a criminal before his Judge, a sinner before his God, a prisoner before his liberator, a slave before his redeemer, a sick man before his physician, a poor man before his benefactor, a friend before the best of friends, and so on, but above all, as a child before its father: such is the doctrine of the Divine Master and of the Holy Ghost.

137. When the Apostles said to their divine Master: "*Domine, doce nos orare,* Lord, teach us to pray" (Luke XI, 1.), it was not their intention to ask for a formula of prayer, but for the manner of praying and speaking to God. Our Lord, in giving a formula of vocal prayer, pointed out the mental dispositions he wishes to find in us. What, then, is this principal disposition? It consists in having the sentiments of a little child towards its father: "*ait illis: Cum oratis, dicite: Pater. ...*and he said to them: When you pray, say: Our Father..." (Luke XI, 2.) Take notice, the intention of our Lord is positive: whenever he gives an instruction on prayer, he wishes that prayer be the request of a child to its father, or the familiar conversation of a child with its father: "*Ora Patrem tuum in abscondito;* pray to thy Father in secret." (Matt. VI, 6.) "*Scit Pater vester quid opus sit vobis, antequam petatis eum;* for your Father knoweth what you stand in need of, before you ask him." (Matt. VI, 8.) "*Pater tuus qui videt in abscondito,* thy Father, who seeth in secret." (Matt. VI, 18.) "*Scit enim Pater vester quia his omnibus indigetis,* your Father knoweth that you have need of all these things." (Matt. VI, 32.) "*Quanto magis Pater vester qui in cœlis est, dabit bona petentibus se!* How much more will your Father, who is in heaven, give good things to those that ask him!" (Matt. VII, 11.)

138. It is the Holy Spirit himself who produces these dispositions

in us: "*In quo* clamamus: Abba, Pater; whereby we cry: *Abba,* *(Father)."* (Rom. VIII, 15.) "*Quoniam autem estis filii, misit Deus Spiritum Filii sui in corda vestra clamantem: Abba, Pater* and because you are sons, God hath sent the Spirit of his Son into your hearts, crying; *Abba, Father."* (Gal. IV, 6.) Behold in God your Creator, your Master, your King, your Judge; be well convinced that you are unworthy of appearing before him; remind him, nevertheless, that he is your Father, and tell him that you are his child, that you do not merit to bear this beautiful name, even not to be reckoned among his servants; but still conclude, like the prodigal Son, saying in all the sincerity of your heart: "*Pater, peccavi,* Father, I have sinned." Let that be if you like, the invariable beginning of all your meditations. Guided by the Spirit of Jesus Christ, the Church addresses the same invitation to us, and I know of no better formula of introduction to meditation than this prayer of the Sacred Liturgy: "*Oremus: Præceptis salutaribus moniti, et divina institutione formati, audemus dicere: Pater noster.* Let us pray: Instructed by thy saving precepts, and following thy divine institution, we presume to say: *Our Father.*"

139. After all this, what is mental prayer? It is the family duty, the duty of every day, which a well-bred child will never consent to neglect; it is the moment when the child comes to converse with its brothers and other members of the family, but especially with its father; it comes to render him its homage, to listen to his words, to promise him filial submission, to assure him of its devotedness, to expose to him its necessities and fears, to discover its weaknesses to him, to await his counsels, and ask him for help and assistance.

140. With this disposition, everything will succeed; without it, you will be checked at every step, for God requires humility and confidence on your part; he wishes that mental prayer be the conversation of the family, "*familiare cum Deo colloquium*" (St. Gregory Nazianzen); he wishes it to be the complete abandonment of the child into its father's hands: "*Oratio est qua cum Deo loquimur, qua Patrem eum dicimus, qua universa nostra desideria in conspectu majestatis ejus effundimus.* Mental prayer is an exercise in which we converse with

God, call him Father, and lay open all our desires before his majesty."
(St. Augustine.)

141. This affectionate, simple, frank, artless, unstudied confidence
is inseparable from every good meditation; because God, as our
Father, is more sensitive to the confidence we place in him, than to all
our other homages. "We are mistaken, if we imagine that to converse
with God very confidentially and familiarly, is want of respect
towards his infinite majesty... Not only is he not displeased thereat,
but he loves to be treated with all that liberty and tender affection
shown by children towards their mothers." (St. Alphonsus Liguori.)

142. Besides, this confidence itself varies in its expressions,
according to the individual character of every one: the serious man
speaks to him with a certain air of gravity; the affectionate soul pours
more unction into her words; the penitent soul intermingles with
them sentiments of regret; the pure heart gazes more directly upon
God; all will speak freely to him, because he is our Father, and
because we all have, even with our many defects, the liberty of the
children of God.

143. The act of faith in the presence of God is of an inexhaustible
fertility; to speak the truth, all the acts which form mental prayer are
founded on faith, have their principle in faith, and derive therefrom
all their force. "Faith," says Suarez, "introduces us to God, and whatever afterwards constitutes true meditation has its roots in faith."

144. Those acts following naturally upon the act of faith in God's
presence, and forming, as it were, but one with it, are the acts of faith
in the various attributes of God, in his supreme majesty, his infinity,
his sovereignty, his eternity, his wisdom, his goodness, his power, his
admirable providence, his justice, his sanctity, his mercy: then in his
works, the Creation, Redemption, Sanctification, etc.; and, lastly, in
whatever he has done in particular for every one of us.

145. These acts are transformed immediately and without effort
on our part, but especially without effort of the head or imagination,
into acts of admiration, humility, annihilation, respect, submission,
gratitude, contrition, fear, hope, confidence, invocation, love, oblation, sacrifice, and holocaust of our entire being. All these acts consti-

tute the supreme act, the homage, reserved to God alone, and perpetually renewed by the saints, the act of *adoration.*

146. "To sum up, all these acts revolve around two truths: God is all, and I am nothing. To exercise our faith in these two truths, to listen to the inspirations of the Holy Spirit in their regard, constitutes all that is comprised in the exercise of the presence of God." (Father Chaminade.) It is also the entire act of adoration; it is the annihilation, the oblation, the sacrifice of ourselves before the infinite majesty of God; it is the most complete homage of which we are capable; it is, therefore, already meditation, and even perfect meditation. It is not astonishing that simple and sincere hearts, as well as generous and heroic souls, find delight in these acts.

147. The act of adoration, inspired and sustained by a vivid faith in the holy presence of God, may be indefinitely prolonged, according as we spend more or less time on one or the other act, or on a great number of those complimentary acts which we have enumerated. Many devout and holy persons are content, in the exercise of meditation, with thus keeping themselves in the presence of God, and feel that they are under the direct regard of this sovereign Majesty, as if they were alone in the world with God. This is sufficient for them; and why should they seek God, when they have found him? Why should they look for a subject of conversation, when God, in his condescension, has taken the initiative, by addressing them first, and discovering his wonders to them?

148. "In mental prayer, we draw nigh to God, and place ourselves in his presence for two principal motives. The first is, that we may render unto God the homage and honor due to him, which does not require that we speak to him, nor that he speaks to us; this duty is fulfilled when we acknowledge that he is God and that we are vile creatures, and thus remain prostrate before him in spirit, waiting for his orders. How many courtiers there are who go a hundred times into the presence of the king, not to speak to him, nor to hear him, but simply to be seen by him, and to testify by this assiduity that they are his servants! And this motive of presenting ourselves before God, solely to lay our will prostrate before him and to testify unto him our

utter devotion to his service, is very excellent, very holy, and very pure, and is, consequently, of a very great perfection."

149. "Our second motive in appearing before God is that we may speak with him and hear him speak unto us by his inspirations and interior movements. This is ordinarily accompanied with a most delicious pleasure because it is a great good to us to speak to so great a Lord. And when he answers, he diffuses a thousand balms and precious ointments, which impart great sweetness to our love for him."

150. "Now," he remarks, "one of these two goods can never fail us in mental prayer. If we can speak to our Lord, let us do so; let us praise him, beseech him, listen to him. If we cannot speak to him because we are hoarse, let us, nevertheless, abide in his apartment and do him reverence. He will see us there; he will kindly accept our patience and favorably look upon our silence. At another time, we shall be amazed when he will take us by the hand, converse with us, and make a hundred turns with us in the garden of his meditation. And if he should never do this, let us be content that it is our duty to belong to his suite, that it is still a great grace and too high an honor if he suffers us in his presence."

151. "Thus we shall not be too eager to speak to him, since the second manner of being with him will not be any the less useful to us, but rather far more so, though perhaps not so agreeable to our taste. When therefore you appear before our Lord, speak to him, if you can; if you cannot, abide there, make him see you, and be not anxious about other matters." (St. Francis de Sales.)

152. "In the palaces of kings and princes," continues St. Francis de Sales, "there are statues which serve only to gratify the eyes of the king; be content to serve a similar purpose in God's presence; he will animate this statue when it shall please him. If a statue, which has been placed in a niche or in the midst of a hall, had the power of speech, and were asked the question 'Why art thou here?' - 'Because,' it would reply, 'the statuary, my master, has placed me here.' - 'Wherefore dost thou not move?' - 'Because he wills that I should remain immovable.' - 'Of what use art thou there? What advantage

dost thou derive from being thus stationary?' - 'It is not for my own service that I am here; it is to serve my master and fulfill his commands.' - 'But thou dost not see him?' - 'No,' the statue would reply, 'but he sees me, and takes pleasure in knowing that I am where he has placed me.' - 'But wouldst thou be glad to have the power of moving, in order to go near him?' - 'Not unless he commanded me to do so.' - 'Desirest thou then nothing?' - 'No, for I am where my master has placed me, and his good pleasure is the only contentment of my being.' Oh, God! It is indeed a good meditation, that of keeping one's self in his will and in his good pleasure. It is my opinion that St. Mary Magdalen was a statue in a niche, when seated at the feet of our Lord, without saying a word, without moving, and, perhaps, without looking at him, she listened to what he said: when he spoke, she listened; when he ceased to speak, she ceased to listen, and nevertheless she was always there. A little infant on the bosom of its sleeping mother is truly in a desirable place, though the mother says not a word to it, nor the child to its mother."

153. When St. Mary Magdalen, in the Pharisee's house, washed the feet of Jesus with her tears, she said nothing, she did but weep over her sins and love; and our Lord said to her: "*Remittuntur ei peccata multa, quoniam dilexit multum.* Many sins are forgiven her, because she hath loved much." (Luke VII, 47.) And Mary, at the foot of the Cross, did not utter a word, and yet it was especially in this moment that she cooperated in the work of our redemption. "They are blessed, O my God," let us say with the Holy Ghost, they are blessed, thy servants who stand before thee always and hear thy wisdom. "*Beati viri tui et beati servi tui, qui stant coram te semper, et audiunt sapientiam tuam.*" (III Kings X, 8.) To remain in the presence of God with a docile and attentive heart, to contemplate him with admiration, to be inebriated with his joys, is not this the life and happiness of the angels? It is also the portion of the pious soul during meditation. The only difference is that the contemplation, or direct vision, is temporarily substituted in us by the indirect vision of faith; but it must be observed that this vision becomes clearer in proportion as our faith increases in vivacity.

154. "Do not fear therefore to stop at the threshold the moment you come in the sight of God; remain there as long as faith keeps your attention fixed, and grace attracts your heart that it may find in God a substantial nourishment and the source of the sweetest consolations." "*Dominus vobiscum*" is the customary salutation of God's minister; "*Deus enim erat cum illo,* God was with him," is the ordinary eulogium of the Holy Ghost when speaking of the patriarchs; "*Dominus tecum*" is the reason why Mary, according to the testimony of the Archangel Gabriel, is full of grace and blessed amongst women; finally the happiness of the saints consists in their being with God. You see that there is nothing more to be desired when we are with God and God is with us. Be with God in meditation, and he will be with you in your actions.

155. "*Sursum corda!*" is the word which your guardian angel will address to you when you are about leaving this visible world to enter into meditation. "*Habemus ad Dominum!*" you reply in union with your brothers. "*Gratias agamus Domino Deo nostro,*" again continues your guardian angel. "*Dignum et justum est.*" And after this response, you continue with one voice: "*Vere dignum et justum est, æquum et salutare, nos tibi semper et ubique gratias agere, Domine sancte, Pater omnipotens, æterne Deus....*" Unite with the angelic choirs: the Dominations, the Powers, the Thrones and Virtues of Heavens, the Cherubs and Seraphs, and solicit permission to join your voice with theirs while saying over and again: "*Sanctus, Sanctus, Sanctus, Dominus Deus Sabaoth....*" Can you do anything better than imitating the angels? But, above all, let faith show God to you with the same certainty, if not with the same clearness, as the Angels behold him. He is with you, he is within you, he is not secluded within the profoundest heavens. Speak to him also by direct address; meditation will become a tête-à-tête, or rather an address to the heart, whenever you preserve a lively faith in the presence of God; nothing is better able to keep up a respectful attention, to favor pious aspirations, and to stir up the noblest impulses of the soul.

156. Be not troubled if these preliminary acts are sometimes prolonged until the moment of the conclusion; you will have made

an excellent meditation, according to the testimony of St. Francis de Sales. It is called by Rev. Father Chaminade "the prayer of faith and of the presence of God."

157. If meditation is made before the Most Holy Sacrament, the act of faith in the presence of God and the complementary acts may be directly addressed to the Sacred Person of our Lord. This circumstance singularly contributes to render these acts more vivid and even easy by striking our mind more forcibly and moving our heart more deeply; it is then that remembering the words of the preface of the Mass, we add: *Per Christum Dominum nostrum;* then we dwell on the goodness our Lord has shown us in the Holy Eucharist, on the mystery we celebrate on that day, or in that period of the year.

158. Let us conclude with the words of St. Francis de Sales: "Being in meditation, Philothea, if you feel your heart attached to the simple presence of God, you will not go farther, but pause at this presence; though you be there, you will gently meditate on the subject you have prepared...; the secret of secrets in meditation is to follow the attractions with a simple heart."

159. This remark of St. Francis de Sales is of the highest importance; it ought to forewarn us against every false or dangerous interpretation of what he has said on the prayer of the presence of God. Meditation is not, under whatever form it may be made, in any case, a special form of indolence or a disguised idleness; consisting essentially of an act or a series of interior acts, it always requires that the soul be acting. Even should she be called to perform the office of a statue, according to the picturesque expression of St. Francis de Sales, you would grossly deceive yourself were you to allow your soul to remain inactive, in a state of supineness, doing nothing, attempting nothing, thinking of nothing. Be statue-like by your docility in allowing God to act freely, in following the attractions of grace; but to follow the attractions of grace is to do something: it is, at least, adds St. Francis de Sales, trying to meditate calmly on the point or subject of meditation.

160. If you wish to be preserved from every dangerous illusion, examine the fruits of your meditation. Have you, after it, a great zeal

for virtue, horror for sin, charity for your neighbor, hatred for yourself and your defects? Do you endeavor to practice humility, obedience, abnegation, courage, and patience in difficulties and in your daily crosses? Be assured, your meditation is excellent: do you not recognize the tree by its fruits?

161. As to the exterior bearing and attitude of the body, he who takes part in a public prayer must conform to the liturgical prescriptions by remaining either kneeling, sitting, or standing. He who prays in private is guided by reverence towards God and by the sentiments of his heart; he will not neglect the exterior means which can aid him in a better acquittal of this pious duty. According to circumstances, he is kneeling, standing, sitting, or walking, in the oratory or in the open air, joining his hands, extending the arms, bowing the head, or raising the eyes towards heaven. Lastly, he will either observe a profound silence, or his lips will give utterance to the abundance of his heart by repeated invocations. He who forms part of a community does not enjoy the same liberty; he must conform to the established customs. The prescriptions of the rule point out to him the will of God, even in details which are purely material and exterior. Thus, all is done with order, uniformity, modesty, respect, and simplicity, without constraint, affectation, and singularity.

162. The exterior bearing must not be looked upon as indifferent, since we pray by our attitude as well as by our entire person; it must even be observed that the attitude of the body greatly influences the sentiments of the soul: "Those," says St. Augustine, "who, in prayer, bend the knee, extend their arms, prostrate themselves, or manifest some other exterior sign of devotion, do what is proper to supplicants. God undoubtedly knows the interior and invisible desires of their heart, and stands not in need of these sensible signs to behold what is going on in the soul; but through these signs man is animated to pray with greater humility and fervor: and just as these movements of the body could not be produced unless preceded by the sentiments of the soul, so likewise, I know not how, the interior and invisible sentiment of the soul is found to increase by the exterior movements of the body."

163. Let us hear St. Francis de Sales insist on this point: "We must be very respectful while addressing the divine Majesty, since the angels, though so pure, tremble in his presence. But, you will say, we cannot have in our meditations this feeling of his presence, which causes such a profound humiliation of all the faculties of the soul, nor that sensible reverence which keeps us low and humble before God, in the knowledge of our littleness and unworthiness. For that very reason, I do not mean to speak of this feeling, which is not necessary; it suffices to have this reverence in the will and the superior part of our soul which should know the sovereign dignity of him whom it loves and adores. In our private meditations and prayers, we must always preserve great respect, since we are in the presence of God, though at the common offices we ought to give it special attention, on account of the edification due to our neighbor; besides, it is certain that exterior reverence is of great assistance to the interior. At all events, that posture is the best which brings with it the greatest attention: yes, even that of lying prostrate is good, and seems to pray of itself; do you not behold the holy man Job, lying on dunghill, saying a prayer so excellent, that it merited to be heard by God?"

164. "The soul, prostrate before God, easily draws the body along with her; she raises the eyes, or the heart and hands to whence she expects help. Do we not see this variety of affections in the countenance of the publican? To say the truth, the essence of prayer lies in the soul; but the voice, actions, and other exterior signs by which it expresses what is within, are noble appurtenances and very useful qualities of meditation. They are its effects and operations: the soul is not content with praying, if the whole man does not pray at the same time; she obliges the eyes, hands, and knees to pray with her. To pray in spirit and truth is so far from praying without ceremonies that, on the contrary, it is scarcely possible to pray in spirit and truth without any actions and exterior gestures in accordance with the interior affections. A soul that is moved is moved throughout: in the tongue, eyes, and hands. To pray in spirit and truth is to pray with the heart and with affection, without pretense or hypocrisy, employing,

besides, thereto the entire man, body and soul, in order that what God has joined may not be separated."

165. Let us conclude with a consideration still more elevated, likewise taken from St. Francis de Sales: "Our Lord himself as man does not abstain from abasing himself profoundly in presence of his Father, by addressing him with extreme reverence, with such acts of profound humility, as never a creature could or was able to do."

IN WHAT THE PRINCIPAL PART, CALLED THE "BODY OF MEDITATION" CONSISTS, AND HOW THE SUBJECT OF MEDITATION IS NATURALLY DIVIDED INTO SEVERAL POINTS

166. The body of the meditation is the intercourse of the soul with God, properly so-called. The subject of this intercourse is precise, and its end is definite, as we have previously remarked. If the subject is read to the community, we should listen with attention; if we meditate privately, we may read it in parts and at intervals; when the subject is sufficiently known, it suffices to recall it to mind summarily.

167. After the immediate preparation, our first act should be to recall to mind the object as well as the end of the audience. Recalling to mind the object is termed by some authors *first prelude,* and that of the end or fruit we have in view, *second prelude.*

168. The object is either a truth, fact, or a mixed subject. We do not speak of virtue, because it is a truth put into practice, and whatever will be said of the considerations on a truth may be applied to considerations on a virtue. The truth is furnished or at least confirmed by the teachings of faith; we should never fail to look for the practical consequences which flow therefrom and find their application in our life. The fact is ordinarily taken from the life of our Lord, of the Blessed Virgin, and of the saints, from Church history, or even from profane history and the ordinary life, but it is always

considered in the light of faith and in the application to our moral conduct.

169. In the following explanations, it is generally understood that the subject of meditation is a truth; later on, we shall see that the same rules are applicable when the subject is a fact or a mixed subject. To understand our counsels and indications more easily, we invite you to make an immediate application of them on a determined subject; you may choose, for instance, prayer, or any virtue whatsoever: obedience, humility; or one of the four last things of man, a great truth of our religion: death, sin; or filial piety towards Mary, love for our Lord, his Passion, etc.

170. The subject of the intercourse having been recalled to mind as we have just said, the soul keeps her attention fixed thereto, and concentrates her faculties, in order to see it in its true light, i.e. in the ensemble and the details, by the simultaneous light of reason and faith. But the power of the mind is limited; when it embraces a vast horizon or a complicated subject, all is vague, obscure, and confused; things become more clear as the forces of our mind are concentrated on a more restricted point, and as we pass successively from one point to another; for a truth is generally an ensemble of truths: a fact, an ensemble of facts; a picture, a complete scenery. For this reason, the division into several points is generally necessitated.

171. Thus in meditation, as well as in every application of the soul to any object whatever, you naturally divide this object into several parts in order to observe them one after the other. Books on meditation ordinarily give the subject as divided into two or three points; but you must not regard yourself as confined to these divisions; their object is to aid you, and not to deprive you of your liberty to adopt others that might present themselves to your mind, whether you consider the subject successively under different aspects, or decompose it by analysis, or simply pass from one idea to another, by following the terms of each proposition. But, I repeat, never torment yourself on account of these divisions. By what is still to be said on the different parts of meditation, you will thoroughly understand how easy it is to divide every subject into several points.

172. While considering the subject, or one of its special points, endeavor, at first, to know it summarily; afterwards consider successively the essential elements, accessory parts, excellence, advantages, and duties it imposes, the difficulties it presents, the means at your disposal, and its application to what concerns you personally.

173. According to the nature of the object which the soul has chosen, and the end she proposes to herself, she applies her faculties to this object differently and devotes herself to distinct operations. If, for instance, it is a question of filial confidence to the Blessed Virgin, the soul may endeavor first to discover the motives thereof, count and weigh them; then recall to mind memorable examples, remaining in admiration at the view of these proofs of the power and goodness of Mary; lastly, we may purpose to preserve constantly this unshaken confidence, which has never deceived anyone, and set about at once, i.e. during the meditation, to make fervent invocations.

174. While observing the numerous operations of the soul, it has been found that all can be classified into three orders or categories: some are referred to the *mind* and other intellectual faculties; others to the *heart*, to the affective faculties or sensibility; and the third to the *will*. Hence, there are three faculties or chief powers of the soul: *intelligence*, *sensibility*, and *will*, wherein all other faculties are comprised. Thus, memory, judgment, and imagination are intellectual faculties; love and hatred, attraction and aversion, derive from sensibility, and are attributed to the heart; finally, deliberate desires, resolutions, and firm purposes derive from the will. When we say that the soul acts, works, we mean to say that she applies her three faculties, or at least one of them, to an object she has in view.

175. Meditation is an operation of such elevated an order that the soul finds application therein for all her faculties. Besides, does not God merit that we be entirely his, when he puts himself at our disposition? All the faculties of the soul are therefore brought into action; the understanding observes, seeks, investigates, discovers; the memory displays whatever refers to the subject, whatever has been previously discovered by the intelligence; the imagination pictures things as present; reason even shows us what is beyond the direct

vision of the soul; the heart is affected, moved, shaken, and thus acting on the soul draws it along; finally, solicited by the mind and heart, the will takes delight in these operations, and transforms the conclusions which have been submitted to it into resolutions.

176. Thus, meditation consists of acts which bear relation to the three principal faculties; it is customary to call the acts of the intellectual faculties *considerations;* what is attributed to the sensibility and heart, *affections;* and what belongs to the immediate domain of the will, *resolutions.* Meditation, according to Rev. Father Olier, consists in the threefold exercise of beholding Jesus, of uniting and of working with him. We behold him in the considerations, we unite with him by our affections, and finally, we operate with him by the accomplishment of the resolutions.

177. The considerations, affections, and resolutions follow in the order in which we have enumerated them, but not exclusively; they are closely connected with one another, intermingle with one another, mutually aid and succeed one another, and return during the exercise of meditation. You will easily understand that it ought to be so, when we shall have explained what you must do and observe in the different parts of the body of meditation.

9

HOW TO MAKE THE CONSIDERATIONS, AND IN WHAT THE "PRAYER OF MEDITATION" CONSISTS

178. The introduction to mental prayer, such as we have explained it, is about to be embodied with meditation itself; we have therefore called it the *prayer of faith* and *presence of God;* it is a prayer in which the acts of faith in the presence and other attributes of God predominate. We are now approaching the subject of mental prayer, and commence to study this subject in the light of faith and reason, and in the presence of God. When this study, such as we are going to explain it, occupies the principal place in the exercise, we have what is called the *prayer of meditation;* it is sometimes designated by the simple name of *meditation.*

179. In meditation, we ought especially to study the truths in the light of faith, i.e. consider them such as faith shows them to us, and give them our adherence in order to make them the rule of our thoughts, judgments, appreciations, and determinations. "As the tincture is gradually imbibed by the linen," says Fenelon, "so should we, for a long time, be penetrated with the truths of the Gospel; they must become familiar to us, that by force of beholding them close to us and at every instant, we may accustom ourselves to judge everything only by them; that they may be our only light in practice, as the

rays of the sun are our only light for perceiving the figure and color of bodies."

180. In meditation, we should especially interrogate faith, because faith alone can instruct us about the things which it imports us to know well, and because the light of faith acts at once on our intelligence, heart, and will. Like the sun's rays which not only illuminate, but also fertilize nature, so the light of faith spreads with vivid brightness in our minds; at the same time, it vivifies the heart and moves the will towards truth and good, thus making every virtue germinate and grow. Reason alone, like the feeble glimmering of a lamp, could not produce the same effects.

181. We should not, however, neglect the light of reason, because it is likewise a gift which God bestowed upon us as a light in our duties. Our intellectual faculties serve us, in meditation, to consult our memory, establish comparisons, draw conclusions, multiply investigations and reflections, etc.; reason and faith mutually assist each other.

182. The meditation of the subject is always useful, often necessary, especially when the subject is one of the great truths of our holy religion: as, the end of man, eternity, sin, death, judgment, hell, heaven, etc. "The eternal truths," says St. Alphonsus Liguori, "are things altogether spiritual, which cannot be conceived with the corporal eyes, but with the eyes of the spirit only, i.e. by thought and reflection. Those persons that do not practice mental prayer, do not therefore see into these truths; this is why they have no idea of the importance of salvation nor of the means they must take to arrive thereat. Thus the loss of so many souls proceeds from their neglecting to consider the importance of the great affair of eternity, and what they must do to save themselves. '*Desolatione desolata est omnis terra, quia nullus est qui recogitet corde;* with desolation is all the land made desolate, because there is none that considereth in his heart.'" (Jer. XII, 11.) The Lord assures, on the contrary, that he will never fall into sin, who directs the eyes of his soul towards the truths of faith; as, death, judgment, a happy or an unhappy eternity which

awaits us: "*Memorare novissima tua et in æternum non peccabis.*" (Eccl. VII, 40.)

183. Why does man live in such utter carelessness, especially in what concerns his soul and those serious questions about his origin, his end, his true dignity and happiness? Why does he remain in ignorance about himself? It is only because he does not deign to stop at the consideration or at the study of these questions.

184. Why is God valued so little in the thoughts of individuals, of nations, and of those that govern? He is *all* and is considered as *nothing;* he is, despite our forgetfulness of his rights, the Master, who has the first and last word everywhere; why do we not see it? It is our want of reflection that produces this blindness.

185. Why do most Christians make so little account of their dignity as children of God, as brothers and co-heirs of Jesus Christ, as temples of the Holy Spirit, as sanctuaries of the adorable Trinity? Because they have never sounded these ravishing mysteries by meditation, and because these words are for them void of meaning; behold why that which is most honorable is least sought for and esteemed.

186. Why is Jesus Christ himself, the incarnate Wisdom, our only and true Master, our light, our guide, and universal hope, so little known, loved, heard, and consulted? Why are the Holy Eucharist and the Sacrifice of the Mass so despised in the world, and often so neglected even in religious communities? The answer is always the same: "*quia nullus est qui recogitet corde!*" Because no one thinks, reflects on these wonders.

187. Why is the Gospel read and studied less than so many profane books by the majority of Christians? Why is it cited and consulted by them so rarely for the guidance of their life? "*Quia nullus est qui recogitet corde!*" They have no idea of the treasures contained in this book of life.

188. Why do men not fear sin, judgment, and hell? "*Quia nullus est qui recogitet corde!*" Why are they obstinate in following the maxims of the world, since their falsehood has been proved for thousands of

years? For the experience of centuries confirms this assertion of St. James: "*Non est ista sapientia, desursum decendens; sed terrena, animalis, diabolica; for this is not wisdom, descending from above; but earthly, sensual, diabolical.*" (James III)

189. In a word, why are men, even Christians, in their ordinary conduct, so light-minded, so thoughtless, so unreasonable, so inconsequent, so foolish, so absurd, as to make one shudder? Why do they allow themselves to be guided in their conduct by prejudices and current opinions, by the wind that blows, by the allurements of blind passions and by human respect? Why do they so often show themselves neither men nor Christians? "*Quia nullus est qui recogitet corde!*" They consult neither reason which constitutes us men, nor faith which makes us Christians. They do not meditate, for in meditation we make use of these two lights, faith and reason. In meditation we discover truth, dispel illusions, and escape from error.

190. Would to God that this light may not shine too late for us, and that we be not obliged, on entering into eternity, to utter this cry of despair, a terrible homage to the wisdom of the saints: "*Ergo erravimus!* We have then erred!" We pitied those who, each day, devoted an hour to meditation, and now do we see them among the number of the children of God, whereas we became wearied on the ways of error and iniquity.

191. One single truth constantly meditated upon would suffice to make us wise and lead us to our end: a proof thereof is St. Francis Xavier, who made as his own the following maxim: "What doth it profit a man if he gain the whole world and suffer the loss of his own soul?" A proof of it is likewise St. Aloysius Gonzaga, who often asked himself this question: "*Quid hoc ad æternitatem?* Of what use will this be to me for my eternity?"

192. St. Augustine asks how we can avoid this abyss which engulfs mankind: "Woe to thee, O torrent of custom among men! Who will stop thy impetuous drift? When wilt thou be dried up? How long yet shalt thou draw the unhappy children of Eve into this immense and formidable ocean? *Væ tibi, flumen moris humani! Quis resistet tibi?*

Quandiu non siccaberis? Quousque volves Evæ filios in mare magnum et formidolosum?" (Conf. I, 16.) St. Augustine answers by his example and teachings: it is only the meditation of the great truths that can constitute our fulcrum and force in the victorious struggle against this torrent.

193. In fine, we repeat: without meditation we can be neither men nor Christians; with the persevering practice of meditation we shall infallibly come to conduct ourselves as men and Christians.

194. We have nothing else to add for recommending to you the daily practice of meditation properly so-called, and to give you an esteem for this part of mental prayer which we have called the *considerations*. But you will say, it is not easy, and not given to everyone to make considerations.

195. Drive from your mind as a temptation of the spirit of lies the thought that you cannot make *considerations* on account of your levity and inconstancy, the want of your mental or intellectual formation. The least cultivated mind can do what God asks of us in meditation. And really, St. Francis of Paula, St. Francis of Assisi, St. Catherine of Siena, St. Teresa of Jesus, St. Rose of Lima, St. Mary Magdalen of Pazzi, and a host of others have arrived at the most sublime degrees of meditation without ever having studied human sciences.

196. Remember especially the example of St. Felix of Cantalice, who died in 1597. This saint passed the first twenty-eight years of his life in directing the plow and keeping flocks; he afterwards joined the Order of Capuchins, in which he filled the office of questant for forty years, going, during the greater part of each day, from house to house, through the streets of Rome. For all his instruction, he had learned the principal mysteries of our holy religion, and knew by heart the *Pater, Ave, Credo,* and *Gloria Patri.* By saying these prayers and reflecting on what he had been taught about our holy mysteries, he elevated himself by and by to the habit of meditation, and to a sublime contemplation. Soon he found, in all he saw and heard, occasions of knowing God better, of admiring and loving him the more; the view of nature had become for him an excellent book of

meditation. But as he progressed, the Passion of our Savior became his favorite book, and he never desisted from reading this book and meditating on its contents. Thus, some vocal prayers which he knew by heart, the things which he saw and heard, the mysteries of religion, and especially the Passion of Jesus Christ: these were the only sources whence St. Felix of Cantalice drew that spirit of meditation, which permitted him to practice this exercise in an easy, continual, and sublime manner, like the angels in heaven. Can you not draw from the same sources? Besides, do your daily imperfections, your numerous sins, not furnish an ample field of matter for the best considerations, that thus you may, at any rate, succeed in avoiding those faults in the future, and in repairing them by penance? Who is the man that has not sufficient intelligence to make this kind of considerations?

197. We are right therefore to repeat with Suarez: "*Nullus est tam ineptus qui non possit ad hoc facile instrui et induci si velit;* no one is so devoid of intelligence, that he cannot easily learn to make meditation, if he only desired it earnestly." Therefore, be at ease; know that no more is asked of you in this part of mental prayer than what you are doing daily in your studies, in your readings, in your mental labors, and even in your conversations with one another. Begin to think about what you are going to speak or to meditate on before God, just as you are obliged to think about what you are going to say in your conversations, and what you are going to do during your studies.

198. Consider, first of all, with the eyes of your mind and in the light of faith, the proposed truth or fact; endeavor to grasp its bearing, to be penetrated with it by reflecting on the meaning of the words which express the subject, distinguish this truth from every other truth, try to sound its depths, to seize its import, to imprint it on your memory, and above all make frequent acts saying: *Credo,* I believe, it is so. You can already catch a glimpse of what is beautiful, good, useful, and practical in this truth.

199. If your mind is unable to go further, this suffices; we will pres-

ently indicate how, in such a case, you can pass immediately to the affections and resolutions. Ordinarily, however, you will feel yourself able to push on further, and to multiply the considerations on this same point. By reflecting, by consulting your memory, by establishing comparisons, and deducing consequences, you will see the subject in a more brilliant light: according to circumstances, you will grasp its full reality, its extent, sublimity, excellence, beauty, advantages, necessity, diverse applications, and above all, its immediate and personal application.

200. Study this truth in the life of our Lord, who is the model of all sanctity; in the life of the most blessed Virgin and the saints, who are the most faithful copies of this divine model. Then address the following questions to yourself: What have our Lord, the most blessed Virgin, the saints, and especially such a saint, thought of this truth? How have they practiced it? What difference exists between their conduct and mine, regarding this truth? What have I yet to do in order to resemble them?

201. Lay special stress on the motives, which should induce you to practice the truth or maxim on which you meditate. The deeper you are penetrated with these motives, the more your will is prompted to take energetic resolutions. It will then be useful to ask yourself the following questions: What do our Lord and the most blessed Virgin ask of me? Should I have the sad courage to refuse it to them? What advantages shall I find in the practice of this virtue? What have I lost until now in default of this practice? What will befall me if I am unfaithful to it? What shall I wish to have done at the end of my life? Is it not necessary to do now what I then should wish to have done? The replies to these questions will suggest salutary reflections to your mind.

202. Above all, I recommend to you not to theorize without application. As to the considerations, questions, and answers, do not fail, in all of them, to look for the relations of these truths to yourself, to your convictions, to the principles of your conduct, to the actions of your life, in a word, to your present dispositions. What are your actual dispositions concerning this truth? Are you really convinced of

it? Do you love it, or do you feel any repugnance in regard to it? Are you firmly resolved to make it the rule of your judgments, of your appreciations, of your conduct, and this, despite the repugnance of nature?

203. Transport yourself into the past in order to better observe the opposition in your conduct to the teachings of faith and even of reason itself. Only ask yourself: what hidden things, what faults unnoticed at the moment, will be manifested to you by the light of meditation, which is a communication of God's light! "*Ab occultis meis munda me, Domine,* you will say, *et ab alienis parce servo tuo.* From my secret sins cleanse me, O Lord: and from those of others spare thy servant." (Ps. XVIII, 13, 14.)

204. Foresee the future, and ask yourself what you will have to do, that the truth on which you meditate may become the rule of your judgments, appreciations, and conduct? What repugnance will you have to overcome? What occasions to avoid? What faults to struggle against? On what occasions shall you put this truth into practice? What means will you take to conform yourself to it? It is not necessary, nor always possible, to ask yourself all these questions during one meditation; but what always imports you, is that you be penetrated with the truth, and, by reviewing the past and looking forward into the future, to give it a practical application to yourself.

205. How easy and salutary it is for you to acquire a knowledge of yourself in meditation, when you are alone in the sight of God, and in the presence of the prescriptions of his holy Will, as you shall stand alone before his judgment-seat! Thus, true meditation is closely connected with the examination of conscience, be it general or particular. To conclude, make meditation to acquire a better knowledge of yourself, and to become such as God wishes you to be. This work is accomplished by frequent reviews on yourself, by incessant comparisons of what you are with what you ought to be; it likewise finds its place in the other parts, i.e. in the affections and resolutions, for it is one of the most useful occupations during meditation.

206. There exist, besides, rules simple enough which facilitate this work and assist you in finding the developments of which you

are in quest. Put into practice yourself the counsels which you would give to your scholars for a composition, an elementary study, a description, a letter, or a short dissertation: the method and ways of proceeding which you would teach them as proper to lead their minds towards discovering in the principal idea other secondary ideas naturally connected with it; the sources which you would point out to them whence they might, ever and anon, draw collections containing developments for any subject whatever, questions which might be given on any subject, fact, or truth, with answers most appropriate to these questions.

207. These rules constitute a true guide who conducts your soul, and shows her in succession, all the parts, all the sides of the object, one after the other; who, placing you in view of the object, puts questions to you similar to those in this well-known verse: "Quis, quid, ubi, quibus, auxiliis, cur, quomodo, quando?" Who has said or done this? What has he said or done? Where? By what means? Why? How? When? Finally, what conclusion is to be drawn? What resolutions to be taken? What have I to do personally? What obstacles are to be removed? What means to be prepared and employed? How have those acted that obtained success?

208. Definitions are then to be given, enumerations to be made, comparisons to be employed; you will remark similarities, opposites, antecedents, consequents, cause and effect, and a thousand other circumstances. Consult the masters and the documents that can furnish you with information: experience, history, books, the testimony of men and especially that of God.

209. The testimony of God is certainly of the greatest assistance to you in the exercise of meditation. You are in the domain of faith, where God speaks directly to your heart by the unction of the Holy Spirit, where he speaks to you as often as you wish, by the examples and doctrine of his Son, by Scripture, Holy Church, the examples and doctrine of his Saints, finally by the ascetic authors. The field is so vast that it is impossible ever to be restrained in your process.

210. The condition of the man who seeks for light in meditation is therefore infinitely above the condition of the one who seeks for light

in study only. To be in the presence of the Divine Master, to possess the facility of consulting him, of interrogating him at any moment in order to ascertain his thoughts upon everything, is, after the beatific vision of the angels, the best condition for seeing, judging, and esteeming everything according to truth.

211. The human means which we have just pointed out must not be neglected. God, who is the Author of the natural as well as the supernatural order, who has grafted faith on reason, and grace on the natural powers of the soul, who employs material elements to produce the wonderful effects, both spiritual and supernatural, of the sacraments, wishes you to have recourse to the natural means according to the measure of your strength, for he neither favors nor approves idleness under any form. Help yourself and Heaven will help you. Exercise yourself then in the processes of which we have spoken, and you will perceive with satisfaction that your mind is rapidly acquiring facility, flexibility, and penetration. You will habituate yourself to grasp promptly and at the first glance the different aspects of an object; little by little you will do instinctively what you have at first done with effort and reflection.

212. But, while applying all the faculties of the soul, be always convinced that the supernatural action is an indispensable help, even for the least success in meditation. Without God's help we can do nothing, absolutely nothing: *"Sine me nihil potestis facere"* (John XV, 5.) Do not therefore omit to ask earnestly for whatever you need. Interrupt the work of the considerations by prayer, multiply acts of faith. Address yourself to God, the Father of lights: to Jesus Christ, his Son, the way, the truth, and the life, the light of the world: to the Holy Spirit, the inspirer of every prayer, without whom all is darkness and impotency; to the most holy Virgin, the seat of wisdom and the channel of all graces; to your guardian angel and holy patrons, your advocates and acceptable intermediaries with God.

213. Have recourse therefore to frequent invocations while applying yourself to considerations; the Holy Scriptures and Sacred Liturgy will furnish you with excellent formulas for this purpose: *"Da mihi intellectum, ut sciam testimonia tua;* give me understanding that I

may know thy testimonies." (Ps. CXVIII, 125.) "*Domine, fac ut videam;* Lord, that I may see." (I Kings, III, 9.) "*Loquere, Domine, quia audit servus tuus;* speak, Lord, thy servant heareth." *Veni, Sancte Spiritus, Et emitte cœlitus Lucis tuœ radium.* Come, Holy Spirit, send us from on high a ray of thy light. *Ave, maris Stella... Solve vincla reis, Profer lumen cæcis.* Hail, star of the sea, break the chains of the guilty, give light to the blind.

214. We must be thoroughly convinced that it is God who gives intelligence and operates all in all... He has shown it in a striking manner in the Apostles and first disciples: "*aperuit illis sensum ut intelligerent;* he opened their understanding, that they might understand." (Luke XXIV, 45); he still shows it each day in simple and humble souls who frequently succeed in making considerations sufficient to produce pious affections and lead them finally to efficacious resolutions.

215. It still remains to warn you against certain dangers. One obstacle, of which many do not think, is to study, instead of meditating and praying, as if we had afterwards to explain and preach these truths to others. This is rather a dissipation through work than a recollection of the soul in prayer. Doubtless we must meditate on our instructions, but it would be imprudent to make a study of meditation. "Although meditation be the investigation of a hidden truth, still its immediate end is not to make us acquainted with new truths of which we have still been ignorant; for its results should be not so much to make us advance in science as to make us progress in the love and devotedness of charity. *Licet meditatio dicatur esse investigatio veritatis occultæ, nihilominus per se non tendit ad cognoscendas novas veritates occultas, quia hæc meditatio non tam ordinatur ad sciendum quam ad amandum et operandum.*" (Suarez.)

216. Avoid also being too eager for grand thoughts and sublime ideas; you would run the risk of passing your time in distractions, of meeting with nothing but dryness, and of gathering deceptions. In meditation, it is out of the question to have curious and nice thoughts; the main thing is to penetrate yourself with a truth in proportion as it is manifested to you in a broader daylight.

217. Take courage then and have confidence! Begin today to make your meditation according to the teachings of your Guide; be faithful to its recommendations, and you will never be stopped nor even embarrassed in that part of meditation which we call *considerations* or *prayer of meditation.*

10

HOW THE AFFECTIONS ARE PRODUCED, AND IN WHAT THE "PRAYER OF SUPPLICATION" CONSISTS

218. In every well-made meditation, the spirit acts on the heart, the considerations re-echo in the sensitive part of the soul, the convictions of the spirit reflect in the heart by attractions or repulsions, and in the will by determinations. How, in fact, can we meditate on hell without being seized with fear at the thought of falling therein; on heaven, without feeling a longing desire to have our abode there; on the Passion of our Savior, without understanding better the value of the soul and the grievousness of sin; on the mission of Mary, without being animated to filial confidence? The more profoundly we meditate on a truth, the more vivid are the sentiments it produces.

219. By the general name of affections, we designate those sentiments which communicate to the soul emotions, inclinations, impulses, sometimes of vigor, sometimes of prostration, which are manifested by love or hatred, fear or confidence, desire or aversion, etc.

220. Affections are sometimes spontaneous; at other times they are voluntary either by nature or in their causes. They are spontaneous when they present themselves without having been sought for; they are voluntary by nature when it is always in our power to produce them: such are the acts of faith, hope, and charity, but espe-

cially the petitions and supplications. They are voluntary in their causes, when we can produce them only in an indirect manner, by reflection; as sentiments of love or hatred, confidence or fear, etc. Both spontaneous and voluntary affections may be kept up and directed by reflection, and thus it is that the affections which are spontaneous by nature are transformed into acts of the will.

221. Behold why in the ascetic language, it is customary to designate, by the name of affections, even those acts in which the will plays often the greatest part, whether by direct intervention, or by the attention kept up in the considerations. These acts, more or less voluntary, consist of aspirations, desires, regrets, prayers, petitions; they are acts of faith, hope, and charity; of humility, contrition, gratitude, admiration, fear, respect, submission, oblation; but most frequently of humble supplications, repeated entreaties, and fervent invocations.

222. The affections vary greatly, and correspond ordinarily to the considerations, which produce them. Thus the considerations on the past call forth acts of humility, fear, regret, gratitude, etc.; the considerations on the present call forth acts of fervor, love, holy desires, etc.; and those on the future call forth acts of hope, confidence, submission to the Will of God, good purposes, etc.; finally, they should all produce humble supplications.

223. "What unites us to God in meditation are not so much the good thoughts of our mind, as the good movements of our will or the holy affections. Now the affections which we produce in meditation are the acts of humility and confidence, of self-denial and resignation, and, especially, those of love." (St. Alphonsus Liguori.) Since these affections depend on the will, it follows that we are always able to produce them.

224. We have just seen how these sentiments are produced and developed by the considerations, but things do not always proceed in this order. St. Francis de Sales says: "We must never check the affections, but allow them to come forth, whenever they present themselves. If, without using violence, your will follows the affections, it is not necessary to play with the considerations; but as this does not

ordinarily happen to us who are imperfect, it is necessary to have recourse to the considerations. Thus, though it be good ordinarily to follow the method, i.e. to introduce the affections after the considerations, the resolutions after the affections, so that the considerations come first; still, if after the mystery has been exposed, the affections find themselves already moved, as it sometimes happens, then the bridle must be slackened, the affections be permitted to have their course, because it is a sign that the Holy Spirit draws us in that direction; for the considerations are made only in order to move the affections."

225. St. Francis de Sales does not even wish the affections to be rejected, if they succeed one another till the end of meditation. "I would lay it down as a general rule that in your meditations you should never check the affections, but allow them to come forth whenever they present themselves until the end of the time appointed for the meditation."

226. It is grace that acts, it is God who speaks to us in the affections which thus come, as it were, of their own accord. "During meditation it is necessary," says St. Vincent de Paul, "to raise the mind to God and to keep ourselves in a humble view of our nothingness, awaiting the moment when God will speak to our heart and say some words of eternal life to us; because one word of his will be productive of greater effects in us than many reasonings and thoughts of our own. Only that which comes from God, only that with which God himself will inspire us, can truly be profitable to our hearts."

227. Therefore, we should never oppose this action of God, i.e., these sentiments of the soul which are betrayed by generous movements, by invocations, cries of admiration, love, and devotion, by ejaculatory prayers: "*In meditatione mea exardescet ignis;* in my meditation, a fire shall flame out." (Ps. XXXVIII, 4.)

228. Still, as the angel of darkness is sometimes transformed into an angel of light, we must be on our guard not to take for a divine operation what may be but a ruse of the demon. There are sensible affections which we must mistrust: they are such as proceed from a purely natural sensibility, and have the only effect of moving our

heart without inducing us to take good resolutions; these kinds of affections lead easily to illusions, as we shall show later on (art. 381).

229. If the sensible attractions we sometimes feel in meditation help us to make meditation well, to deny ourselves, and to practice virtue, they are graces and encouragements which Almighty God sends us and for which we ought to be grateful. But let us always bear in mind that these attractions and consolations are not in our power, that they are neither necessary nor meritorious in themselves, and that we can make excellent meditations without feeling the least pleasure therein.

230. But often it is not sufficient simply to give free scope to these sentiments, and to express them in passing; it even does not suffice to entertain them when they are presented to us under the action of grace; in most cases it is useful and even necessary to call them forth by an effort of the will, to reproduce them, to strengthen them, and to give them more life and energy. Affections which have been thus brought forth, may occupy a greater place in the body of the meditation than the considerations. This has even been counseled and practiced by the masters of the spiritual life, among others by St. Augustine, St. Teresa, St. Francis de Sales, St. Vincent de Paul, and St. Alphonsus Liguori.

231. It is well understood that we speak here of affections, inasmuch as they depend on our will: among these affections, there is one kind which is always in our power, that of supplication, under the most diverse forms. Now the prayer of supplication is the best affection and most useful occupation during meditation.

232. Why do the words *mental prayer*, which signify prayer, petition, supplication, at the same time, designate the considerations, affections, resolutions, and every other act of this holy exercise? Because the prayer of supplication ordinarily occupies the largest place in mental prayer and constitutes its noblest part.

233. "In meditation, it is very useful, and perhaps preferable to all else, to pray frequently, by asking God humbly and confidently for his holy grace, i.e. for the light of which we stand in need, for resignation, perseverance, etc., but especially for the gift of holy love. St.

Francis de Sales has said that with the gift of divine love we obtain every grace. In truth, a soul that really loves God with all her affections will, of her own accord, and without being told, avoid whatever could displease the Lord, and will endeavor to be agreeable to him in all things. If you happen to be subject to dryness and obscurity, to such a degree as to feel yourself unable to produce good acts, it then suffices to say: My Jesus, mercy! Lord, for mercy's sake, help me! Such a meditation may perhaps be the most useful and beneficial to you." (St. Alphonsus Liguori.)

234. Let us conclude these reflections by the following words of the same saint: "The principal fruit of meditation is prayer." This is not a vain tautology; St. Alphonsus thereby declares to us that of all the acts of meditation, the affections merit the preference, and of all the various kinds of affections, the petitions, supplications, and invocations hold the first rank.

235. How consoling it is to state that the most useful act of meditation is at the same time the easiest! Is there any man, no matter in what situation he may be, who cannot say and repeat a thousand times: Father, remember that I am thy child; see, I want this, I need that: besides I am certain that thou wilt grant it to me, since thou hast promised me whatever I should ask of thee, because thou art infinitely good and ever faithful to thy promises, and because thou lovest me. Or further: I am in danger of perdition, save me! I am sick, cure me! I am blind, grant that I may see! I am miserable! O my Jesus, mercy! etc.

236. Is there any condition in life in which this simple prayer is not easy? But the more poor, miserable, and forsaken you are, without hope in any direction, the more favorable is your condition. The more freely ought prayer to ascend from your heart. "There is nothing easier than to pray: Lord, assist me; Lord, help me; grant me thy love, etc. Can anything easier be found?" (St. Alphonsus Liguori.)

237. Let us henceforth attach ourselves to this practice, and we shall experience in ourselves what St. Alphonsus has noticed in the souls which he directed, and which, according to the same saint, was felt by a religious who has become a distinguished master in the spir-

itual life, the venerable P. Segneri: As long as we apply ourselves in meditation principally to reflections, we encounter almost insurmountable obstacles; as soon as we begin to multiply petitions, invocations, and ejaculatory prayers, we progress rapidly with but little trouble.

238. Such is also the practice of Holy Church. Have you already taken notice that almost all the exercises and liturgical offices of our holy religion are composed of short prayers, of simple requests, which follow each other without transition, without interruption, and are often repeated in the same terms and under the same form? You will find it to be so, if for this purpose you peruse the psalms, hymns, versicles, responses, and other parts of the Breviary, all the prayers of the Missal and Ritual, the most ordinary prayer of the Christian, the *Pater, Ave, Veni Sancte, Sub tuum*, grace before and after meals, the Litanies of the Blessed Virgin, of the holy Name of Jesus and of all the Saints. They always consist of short invocations or recommendations addressed directly to God, to the Blessed Virgin, and to the Saints.

239. Make your choice from this rich collection, from Scripture, from the writings of the Saints, and from books of piety; make for your own personal use a collection, like an immense bouquet, or spiritual quiver, wherein you keep a deposit of your ejaculatory prayers; note down likewise, in this spiritual memorandum-book, striking thoughts, pious maxims, and fervent invocations, with which you come across in your pious readings. Then frequently peruse, sometimes one page, sometimes another of this valuable collection; soon you will perceive that you possess an inexhaustible treasure, a source whence gushes forth life-giving water. In your meditation, these texts will freely present themselves to your mind; they will become, without any labor on your part, the expression of your sentiments, the aliment of your affections, the formula of your prayers: you will draw at will these ejaculatory prayers from your quiver to direct them towards heaven under the impulse of your heart.

240. After the example of the Church, be careful to address these prayers to God and to his Saints by employing the direct discourse, by

making your petitions to them without an intermediary, and speaking to them as we do to one before whom we stand. Do not forget that you are in the presence of God and his Saints; for every prayer, whatever be its ulterior character, is at first a prayer of faith and of the presence of God.

241. How easy and eloquent are not these direct invocations: "*Domine doce nos orare; — Domine fac ut videam; Da mihi intellectum; — Deus in adjutorium meum intende; — Kyrie eleison; Jesus, lux vera Jesu, bonitas infinita, misere nobis; — Veni Sancte Spiritus; Sancta Maria salus infirmorum, consolatrix afflictorum ora pro nobis,* etc. Lord, teach us how to pray. Lord, that I may see. Give me intelligence. O God, come to my assistance. Lord, have mercy. Jesus, the true light; Jesus, infinite goodness, have mercy on us. Come, Holy Ghost. Holy Mary, health of the sick, comfort of the afflicted, pray for us."

242. Thus prayed those who had the happiness of enjoying the visible presence of our Lord. Everywhere in the Gospel, you will find that the considerations, the reasonings are short, but the affections and supplications are lively and frequent. Let us but call to mind some examples, whose details you may find in the sacred text. The centurion made use of this short reasoning: "My soldiers and servants obey me at the first word; say but one word and my servant shall be healed." (Matt. VII.) The Canaanite woman makes use of a humble comparison: "The whelps also eat of the crumbs that fall from the tables of their masters": such is her entire statement; but her prayers are so earnest, so importunate, that the Apostles are fatigued by them. (Matt. XV.) The good thief makes likewise a short and simple reflection; the rest of the time, he supplicates the Savior not to forget him when he shall have entered his kingdom. They are accomplished models.

243. Could you ever be embarrassed about what to ask of God? But in that case, you would be the most pitiful of men, because you would be in a profound blindness concerning yourself, your brothers, and the needs of the holy Catholic Church.

244. Consider your personal wants, the interest of those confided to you, your sufferings, weariness, daily deceptions, the persons and

works depending on your zeal. How many subjects of supplicating invocation, of incessant ejaculatory prayers; what an easy, sweet, and useful occupation during your meditations!

245. Place no limits to your affections and desires, and in consequence to your petitions. Has it not been said to us: "*Estote perfecti sicut Pater vester cœlestis perfectus est*: be ye perfect as your heavenly Father is perfect?" (Matt. V, 48.) "We should wish," says St. Philip Neri, "to surpass, if it were possible, even the sanctity of SS. Peter and Paul; we cannot attain such a happiness, but we ought to desire it ardently, that we might accomplish by desire what we cannot accomplish in reality." The *Pater,* this model prayer, is composed, in the first part, of three desires of this kind: hallowed be thy name; thy kingdom come; thy will be done on earth, as it is in heaven! You cannot therefore entertain the least doubt as to the excellence of this manner of praying which we recommend, since it is that of our Lord himself.

246. Is it not equally conformable to the heart of God to multiply invocations in favor of all noble and holy causes: for holy Church, for the society or family to which we belong; for the just, that God may preserve them; for the sinners, that he may pardon them; for the departed, that he may alleviate their pains; for the living, relatives, friends, pupils, benefactors, the afflicted, the sick, the captives, for infidels and heretics, that he may bestow upon them the benefits of his mercy?

247. If you are a member of the Apostleship of Prayer, you will not be able to count the petitioners who crowd around you to ask for the help of your prayers; you will become, according to the title of the Association, an Apostle by prayer, and you will work as effectively at the conquest of souls as missionaries and preachers do by word of mouth. It will be a consolation for you to recall to mind the examples of St. Teresa, St. Mary Magdalen of Pazzi, and so many others who, by their prayers, have converted as many souls as St. Francis Xavier and his numerous followers. Prayer alone obtains more than mere preaching, and even the word of the Gospel owes its force to prayer, which draws the heavenly graces down upon earth.

248. But let us make an almost inadmissible supposition. Let us

admit that you are sometimes reduced to such a state of weakness, powerlessness, prostration, distraction, aridity, and discouragement, that you think it impossible to have, to entertain, and to repeat the least good thought. You will then, at least, not be unable to acknowledge and confess that such is the state of your soul. Now, is not this an act of humility, a wholesome conviction, an avowal far more pleasing to God than a great number of thoughts that would appear to you more worthy and meritorious?

249. Thus, the act of humility is never impossible and becomes easier as, in reality, you are more miserable. What excuse do you still have to allege? What even remains for you to desire in order to be, whenever you wish, a man of prayer?

250. The acknowledgement of your nothingness is at the same time the best exercise and the most desirable effect of meditation. Listen to St. Teresa: "The least act of this virtue, when it takes place in the presence of the Eternal Wisdom, is worth more than all the science of the world. There is then no longer time for reasoning, but for acknowledging sincerely what we are, and presenting ourselves in this condition before God." Imitate the publican who did not dare to lift his eyes towards heaven; for this manner of praying is infinitely more agreeable to God than all the eloquence of rhetoricians and all the science of savants.

251. Thus, when you are stopped for any reason whatsoever and unable to conceive, say, or wish anything, make an act of humility on this very inability and cast yourself into the merciful arms of God. It was the process of that admirable man of meditation, St. Francis of Assisi. He loved in his meditation to repeat this prayer: "My God and my All, who art thou, sweet Lord? What am I, thy servant? A mean worm, I would wish to love thee, most holy Lord, I would wish to love thee. O God, I have consecrated my heart and my body to thee! If I should know how to do still more for thee, I would do it, I desire it ardently." The royal Prophet also had constantly recourse to this kind of prayer. Read the psalms; what recurs most frequently are invocations similar to those composing the two magnificent psalms which we know by heart: *Miserere mei Deus, secundum magnam misericordiam*

tuam. — De profundis clamavi ad te, Domine, Domine exaudi vocem meam.

252. Join confidence to humility, and you will have a perfect meditation; be before God as a child before its father. I refer you again to arts. 136-142; read them again to complete our teaching on this part of mental prayer called affections, or prayer *of supplication;* for, as we have pointed out first the *prayer of faith* and of the *presence of God,* afterwards the *prayer of meditation,* so we now point out the *prayer of supplication;* by this name we designate mental prayer, whenever it is composed principally of those humble prayers and invocations, whose frequent use we have just counseled you. I need not say, of course, that the prayer of supplication is always united to the prayer of faith and of the presence of God, and that it is mostly based on meditation.

253. Remember well that the prayer of supplication is the most wholesome, the most divine, the most useful and delightful occupation, and the easiest of all the exercises of piety. May henceforth your heart seek its repose in this holy exercise! It will find therein that peace which the world cannot give, because therein it will find its God, the source of every consolation.

254. When the heart belongs to God, everything belongs to God; for the heart soon finishes by drawing the will along with it; and with the will all the actions of your life. Accordingly and without our knowledge, our affections become resolutions: they are converted into holy desires, protestations of fidelity, generous promises and firm purposes. It is God who operates these wonders, for he moves the heart, and afterwards still operates on the heart to produce the desire and action: *"inclina cor meum in testimonia tua:* incline my heart unto thy testimonies." (Ps. CXVIII, 36.) *"Deus est enim qui operatur et velle et perficere:* for it is God who worketh in you both to will and to accomplish." (Phil. II, 13.)

255. What is essential and all important for us is to let God act; then place yourself entirely at his disposal, repeating with St. Teresa: "Dispose of me and of all that belongs to me as it pleases thee." The seraphic St. Teresa was accustomed to repeat this act of affectionate

offering more than fifty times a day. Do not therefore tell me any longer that you do nothing during meditation. Great God! What can you do better than expose your misery to your heavenly Father and ask him to have pity on his child? Remember well; it is better to devote yourself to affections than to reasonings. The utility of mental prayer consists less in the meditation itself than in the affections, prayers, and resolutions, which are the three principal fruits of mental prayer.

11

HOW "RESOLUTIONS" ARE FORMED AND IN WHAT THE "PRAYER OF UNION" CONSISTS

256. The mind sees what is to be done, it conceives, designs, and projects; the heart forms desires, the will alone decides the execution of projects and the accomplishment of desires: the decisions of the will are called resolutions.

257. We have seen how resolutions are produced; they have their origin in the considerations: *Ignoti nulla cupido,* according to an old saying; we do not feel, we cannot even feel a desire for what we do not know. Thus, the intelligence shows the object, the heart attaches itself to it or repels it, and the will is the more strongly solicited as the heart is the more vividly affected. Nevertheless, the will is attracted only as far as it gives consent thereto, because it is free, i.e. master of its resolutions and responsible for its acts.

258. God operates upon the will by his grace, as the intellect does by its lights and the heart by its attractions: without the intervention of God, or without the help of his grace, the will would be unable to desire the least good, or to produce any effective resolution, any supernatural act.

259. But if, on the one hand, the will cannot do anything, nor does anything unless enlightened by the mind, attracted by the heart, and

strengthened by grace, the considerations on the other hand will like-wise remain purely theoretical, the affections powerless, and grace sterile, as long as the will does not give assent and command its execution. Thus the action of the will is decisive and necessary. The most beautiful considerations would resemble a utopia, the most ardent affections would be reduced to a phenomenon of sentimen-tality if they did not end in manly and fruitful resolutions.

260. The resolution is the personal and most complete act of meditation. It finishes what has gone before and regulates what is to follow. Good resolutions conduct a man to perfection. If you are not what you ought to be before God and men, it is because up to this day your resolutions were not what they should have been.

261. We have neglected no opportunity to remark that, in an upright and sincere soul, the considerations and affections are rarely produced during the course of the meditation without the will taking, at the same time, some holy determination, some praiseworthy reso-lution. The question is only to be careful that the resolutions do not remain sterile; therefore, it is always useful and often necessary to consecrate some time to this part of mental prayer.

262. But like other acts of meditation, good resolutions are more the gift of God than the fruit of our industry. You should therefore be mindful, whilst you are taking your resolutions, to have recourse to the most earnest supplications: vary the expression of these invoca-tions, make use of ejaculatory prayers, and successively address your-self to God, to the most holy Virgin, to your guardian angel and to your holy patrons. At no time is the help of God more indispensable than when you are about setting to work at your own conversion and sanctification: "Nisi Dominus ædificaverit domum, in vanum labo-raverunt qui ædificant eam; if the Lord does not help, and himself erect the edifice of our sanctity, all those that labor at it will be sadly surprised to learn that their labors have remained fruitless." (Ps. CXXVI.) Renew then your invocations. As soon as a good resolution has been taken, confide its deposit to the most holy Virgin. Is she not the guardian of our treasures; "posuerunt me custodem?" Is she not the singular vessel in which the treasure of our devotion is preserved?

The tower of David, by which we are protected against our enemies? Lastly, the channel of all graces? Our confidence in her ought to be unlimited. "Ipsa enim detinet virtutes ne fugiant, merita ne per eant gratias ne effluant. Mary guards the deposit of our virtues, lest they perish, our merits, lest they be lost, the graces, lest they be wasted." (St. Bonaventure.)

263. Resolutions are like trees; those are good which bear fruit. Nevertheless, as the fruit does not appear immediately or instantaneously, measures have been taken to discern good from false resolutions, by some well-nigh infallible marks. Every good resolution ought to be: 1. Precise, i.e. determined, particular, and to the point. Mark out what is to be done, the time, place, manner, means, etc.; whatever is vague, is impracticable. "It often happens that the means for attaining our salvation, when considered in bulk or in general, are agreeable to our heart; but, when looked at in detail or in particular, they are frightful: this is why in holy meditation, we make special resolutions." (St. Francis de Sales.) "It is necessary, O Philothea," still continues the same Saint, "that you change the general affections into special and particular resolutions for your correction and amendment. For example, take the first word spoken by our Savior on the Cross; it will, doubtless, diffuse a holy affection in your soul, viz., the desire of loving and pardoning your enemies. Now I say to you, that this is of little value if you do not add thereto some special and particular resolution of this kind: Well then, I will no longer be vexed about the angry words that this person, my neighbor, or my servant may speak about me, nor of the contempt that may be shown me by that person; on the contrary, I will do these actions to gain and soften them, and so on of others. By this means, O Philothea, you will correct your faults in a short time."

264. 2. Personal: this quality is comprised in precision; we name it nevertheless, that you may not fail to consult your nature, your past and present life, your future, your experience, your passions, especially your ruling passion, your inclinations, necessities, resources, and duties. "Since you know from what direction the enemy presses

you most, it is there, that you must resist, fortify yourself strongly, and keep on your guard." (St. Francis de Sales.)

265. If you are still a beginner in the spiritual life, and endeavor to correct your faults, commence with the one that seems to be the most dangerous. It is that which ordinarily constitutes our predominant passion, or a sin that is accompanied with scandal, such as the neglect of the duties of our state, slander, disobedience, or criticizing. If you are endeavoring to acquire virtues, commence with the most important, such as humility, obedience, and charity. Of the acts proper to these virtues, apply yourself first to those of a more habitual practice.

266. 3. Actual or proximate; if the resolution has not an immediate application, it has most frequently no application. Sufficient for the day is the evil thereof. Attend to what must be acquired or reformed for the moment, otherwise you will remain in the field of speculation, and nothing will be accomplished. "If, for instance, I have resolved to gain by gentleness the hearts of those who have given me offense, I will try today to meet them that I may offer them a friendly greeting; and if I cannot meet them, I will speak well of them, and pray to God in their behalf." (St. Francis de Sales.) Therefore, say to yourself: Today I will avoid such an occasion where I am liable to fall; will watch over myself especially on that occasion; I will acquit myself of this duty as I should, and to that end, take the following means, etc.

267. 4. Firm, i.e. considered and weighed in the scales of the sanctuary. This resolution ought not to be a mere whim, but a sovereign will, which commands and makes use of the means, a pious will which confides in God and is sure of success, because it joins action to prayer; it is the union of man's will with the holy Will of God; it is therefore also the union of man's weakness with God's strength, the whole is nothing less than the strength of God: *Quis ut Deus?*

268. 5. Persevering or constantly renewed, until a desired result is obtained; it is one of the qualities of firmness. Since the resolution should bear relation to the wants of our soul, it follows that we ought not to take another one every day, and that it is necessary to renew the same one frequently; for it is neither in a few days nor in a few

weeks that we can correct ourselves of a defect, or acquire a good habit. Thus the same resolution may be renewed for weeks, months, and even years. "If we rooted out each year but one vice," says the author of the *Imitation* of *Christ*, "we should soon become perfect." It is therefore prudent to keep to one resolution only, or at least to a very small number of them; the effect will be surer, more rapid, and complete. There are duties in the spiritual life, which may be compared to the exterior works of fortification. Of this number are: fidelity to the exercises of piety, good employment of time, silence of the tongue, etc. As soon as the enemy has effected a breach in one of these outer works, we must hasten to repair it, and direct our resolutions and efforts towards this point. At the close of each meditation take the invariable resolution of being faithful till the next meditation, and to prepare everything to make it well.

269. There is a quality which dominates and comprises all the others, viz. conformity to the Will of God. A thing, whatever it be, is good only because it is according to the will of God, and inasmuch as it is so. We make meditation only to know and execute the Will of God in our regard. We know that for a religious, the Rule is the expression of the Will of God; for the Christian, the commandments of God and of the Church; for all, the duties of their state. "Conformity to the Divine Will is the treasure of the true Christian; it contains, in an eminent degree, mortification, perfect submission, self-abnegation, imitation of Jesus Christ, union with God, and, in general, all virtues, which are such only because conformable to the Will of God, the origin and rule of every perfection." (St. Vincent de Paul.)

270. Conformity to the Will of God is the supreme end, not only of every prayer, but of every exercise, of every act of our life, and of our life itself. On this account, all the parts of mental prayer meet at this last conclusion, and all the kinds and varieties of prayer have their consummation in the prayer of *conformity to the Will of God,* which might also be called the *prayer of union with God.*

271. In fact, nothing can more intimately unite us with God here on earth, than this conformity of the wills; the supernatural union of

grace is in direct relation with the union of the wills, and true perfection is in this union. Every perfection not marked with this stamp is illusory.

272. By the prayer of the union of wills, we become completely the organs of Jesus Christ, the members of his mystical body: "*unum corpus sumus.*" (Rom. XII, 5.) Jesus Christ, acting by us, and in us, acts himself and continues by his members, i.e. by himself, as well as by us, his life, apostolate, teaching, works, and sufferings. Nothing is then more true than this saying of St. Paul: "*Mihi vivere Christus est,* Jesus is my life." (Phil. I, 21.) "*Vivo autem, jam non ego, vivit vero in me Christus.* I live, now not I, but Christ liveth in me. (Gal. II, 20.) Jesus Christ thus becomes all to all, and operates all in all. It is the last term of the Christian's vocation on this earth. Why is this doctrine not more universally meditated upon, preached, and taught?

273. Behold in what words Rev. Father Olier sums up this doctrine: "To work in Jesus is to desire the accomplishment of his divine Will in us, his members, who ought to be submissive to our chief and have no other motion than that which is given to us by Jesus Christ, our king and our all, who, replenishing our souls with his spirit, virtue, and force, should be operating in and by us whatever he wishes. With the pastor, he is Pastor; with the priests, a Priest; with the religious, a Religious; with the penitents, a Penitent; and it is through them that he is to operate the works of their vocation."

274. We cannot go beyond this union of grace and will with our Lord. The Will of God is both the primary reason and the ultimate perfection of whatever exists. It is, consequently, the very perfection of heaven, and the only perfection to be established on this earth: *Fiat voluntas tua, sicut in cœlo, et in terra.* Nothing pleases God so much, nothing draws down upon the soul more abundantly the looks of his benevolence than the dispositions summed up in these words: "*Fiat mihi secundum verbum tuum;* be it done to me according to thy word." "Our Lord communicates himself accordingly to souls who conform themselves unreservedly and constantly to the holy Will of God, and consult only his good pleasure in what they desire or do not desire." (St. Vincent de Paul.)

275. By reason of the very excellence of this disposition, which constitutes the *prayer of union* such as we understand it here, we come back once more on this denomination and on the object thereof. What we call here *prayer of union*, must not be confounded with what, in mystic theology, is designated by the same name. But if the state of the soul is not the same in both cases, if the exterior signs differ sensibly, do not, my dear friend, deduce from this difference any sad or lamentable consequence for yourself, who follow the ordinary and common road. I cannot tell you anything more consoling and more decisive, than the reply our Savior made on a well-known occasion.

276. Our Savior was one day speaking to the multitudes; his mother and relations were there, but could not approach him on account of the crowd. Then one said to him: "Behold thy mother and thy brethren stand without, seeking thee." But he answering him that told him, said: "Who is my mother, and who are my brethren?" And stretching forth his hands towards the disciples, he said: "Behold my mother and my brethren. For whosoever shall do the will of my Father who is in heaven, he is my brother, and sister, and mother." (Matt. XII, 47-50.) It is not, says elsewhere our Savior, the gift of miracles, nor even the gift of prayer, which will one day be rewarded in you, and which today ought to inspire you with some confidence: but your fidelity to conform in all things to the will of your Father, who is in heaven. (Matt. VII, 21-22.)

277. Nothing is superior to the accomplishment of the Will of God; as a consequence, nothing is superior to this *prayer of union*, which consists in the conformity of our will to the supreme will of God, which makes us love and seek this conformity, and aim thereat in all our actions. This prayer of union is the terminus or perfection of all the other kinds of prayer, which we have mentioned, and which might still be indicated. Every prayer, under whatever form it is developed, ends therefore in the prayer of union; if practiced with true simplicity of heart, its effect must necessarily be, even without our mind reverting to it, to dispose our life, whether in the ensemble or in detail, according to the holy will of God.

278. "Hence," do we conclude with St. Teresa, "all that is to be sought after in the exercise of mental prayer, is the conformity of our will with that of God; to be well convinced that herein lies the highest perfection: he who most excels in this practice, will receive from God the greatest gifts, and will progress most rapidly in the interior life."

12

ABOUT THE LENGTH OF TIME TO BE DEVOTED TO THE DIFFERENT PARTS OF MENTAL PRAYER

279. What has just been said of the considerations, affections, and resolutions relates to the first point, truth, or thought which occupied your attention at the commencement of mental prayer. When you find that you have dwelt a sufficient time on this first point, be it that the matter is exhausted for you, or because you feel satiated, pass to the next point and go over the same process again; after which you may pass on to another point, if time permits.

280. But, you may say, how long shall I stop at each point, and besides, how many minutes should I successively devote to the considerations, affections, and resolutions? Although the answer to this question is already contained in preceding chapters, we nevertheless wish to give a direct reply in summing up what has previously been stated.

281. Nowhere should there be at the same time greater docility and liberty than in the service of God; consequently, there is nowhere greater variety than in the practice of mental prayer.

282. Everyone modifies this exercise according to the state of his mind, the disposition of his soul, the inclinations of his heart, and according to numberless circumstances, but, above all, according to the attractions of the Holy Ghost. Today you dwell longer on the

preparatory acts, tomorrow on the considerations, another day on the affections, then again on the resolutions; thus you give to your mental prayer each time another character; and these different acts succeed one another, reproduce themselves, and are blended one with another in all kinds of shapes.

283. Wishing to proceed further, you would like to ask me if it would not be proper, nevertheless, to trace for oneself some precise rules relative to the duration and succession of the different parts of meditation, without, however, adhering too much to the letter. Would it be advisable, for example, in a quarter of an hour's meditation, to devote about one minute to the proximate preparation, four minutes to the considerations, four minutes to the affections, four minutes to the resolutions, and two minutes to the conclusion?

284. Once more we repeat it, preserve the liberty of the children of God. Be not the slave of any process, of any method whatsoever; for the method is to guide you, and not to keep you back. If God himself conducts you, if you advance by following the lights and attractions of grace, why do you look back, or about, to see whether you are walking according to the rules of the method?

285. On this subject listen to our amiable St. Francis de Sales: "Those greatly deceive themselves," says the saint, "who consider that for mental prayer there is required an abundance of methods and certain art which consists, according to them, in subtilizing and refining their meditation, to see how they are doing it, or how they may do it to satisfy themselves, thinking that one must neither cough nor move for fear the Spirit of God should withdraw itself. A great deceit, indeed; as if the Spirit of God was so delicate that it depended on the method and countenance of those who perform the meditation. I do not say that one ought not to use the methods that have been alluded to; but I do say that one ought not to attach oneself to them, as those do who think they have not made their meditation well if they do not place their considerations before the affections given them by God, which latter are nevertheless the end for which we make the considerations. Such persons resemble those who, finding themselves at the place whither they wanted to go, return

again because they had not arrived by the road they had been told to go."

286. Prove by your simplicity, that you are children of God: *simplices filii Dei.* The children who gather about their father, do not study so carefully all their movements and words. If they are what they ought to be, they know how to conduct themselves properly, to be silent when necessary, and to speak at the proper time. Today they speak more, tomorrow they listen longer; another time they simply remain in the father's presence, together with their mother and the other members of the family: they are glad to behold, to be admitted to this beautiful reunion of the family, to belong to it, and to enjoy it. Is not this sufficient to constitute *the prayer of faith and presence of God?*

287. Whenever the Spirit of God diffuses his light over some great truth or some mystery, and strikes your intelligence in such a manner as to keep its attention riveted to the subject, that you may consider it under all its forms, sift it well, and contemplate it at once in its whole extent, and depth, and in its application to your conduct, then obey this spirit, and make a *meditation* or the *prayer of meditation.*

288. Another time this same Spirit of God will, from the beginning, take hold of your heart and supply you abundantly with desires, affections, petitions, wishes, and invocations; or he will leave you to your impotence and cause you to utter cries of distress. Then it is time for you to apply yourself to the *prayer of supplication.*

289. Finally, behold how the will of God appears to you in its sanctity, justice, and loveliness, then in the application to the acts of your daily life; the Holy Spirit will prompt you to holy affections interspersed with pious resolutions; practice then the *prayer of union* or of *conformity to the will of God.* Slacken, hasten, regulate your march under the inspirations of the Holy Spirit, who breathes, when, where, and as it pleases him.

290. What should always be found with you during mental prayer is the habit of having frequent recourse to the invocations; then an absolute docility to the Holy Spirit; finally, the individual labor under the influence of grace; the attention concentrated on the subject meditated upon; the spirit enlightened and convinced by the light of

faith and its own reflections; the heart disengaged from its vanities, and gained over to all that is truly beautiful, just, and holy; the will, the entire man united to the holy Will of God.

291. The method favors personal action as well as the action of the Holy Spirit: in the same meditation it will come to pass that in the second point you neglect the process which has occupied you fruitfully in the first; a little later you will be struck at what, but a moment before, has left you unmoved. Today you will make, above all, the prayer of faith or the presence of God, tomorrow that of meditation, another day the prayer of supplication, or that of union.

13

HOW TO END MENTAL PRAYER, OR HOW TO MAKE "THE CONCLUSION"

292. When mental prayer is made in community, it is customary to give warning by a signal about three minutes before the end, that there are but a few minutes left to finish and take leave. Then break off the conversation in order to make use of these last moments for those acts which the most elementary notions of propriety and your own dearest interests will not permit you either to omit or to perform negligently. These acts correspond to those with which you have commenced your meditation; you may vary them, and you may stop at each as long as time permits, or your soul retains you in a useful manner.

293. Here follow the principles of these acts: 1. The homage of your gratitude or a last thanksgiving, in which you cast a rapid glance over the interview in the light of a signal grace and a mark of God's special benevolence towards you.

294. 2. An act of regret, excuse, sincere confusion at the remembrance of the faults into which you have fallen by reason of your weakness, under the very looks of God, at the very moment in which he opened the treasures of his heart for you. Before terminating this exercise, we must try to repair our faults as much as possible. The Holy Spirit himself invites us never to allow ourselves to finish our

meditation badly: "*Melior est finis orationis quam principium.* The end of prayer is better than the beginning thereof." (Eccles. VII. 9.)

295. 3. A firm purpose which applies to all the resolutions already taken, but principally to the one on which you are going to concentrate all the forces of nature and grace, and one which you will renew until a satisfactory result has been obtained.

296. 4. A maxim or a thought of faith, expressed by a text of holy Scriptures or by a sentence of some saint; this act is a complement of the preceding. This text ought to unite, as it were, and implicitly recall all the good sentiments of the meditation, on which account it is called the *spiritual bouquet.* It is not necessary to change this bouquet at each meditation.

297. 5. A last word addressed to God, to the blessed Virgin, or to some saint on the subject or end of meditation: it is sometimes called *colloquy.*

298. It is a general custom to terminate the exercise by a vocal prayer recited in community. This prayer is a final recourse to our patrons, because we stand in need of their protection and defense after meditation, since we carry such great spiritual riches; on which account we must be on our guard, "acting herein," says St. Francis de Sales, "like a man who has received a liquor of great price and carries it home in a vessel of beautiful porcelain. He walks very gently minding nothing around him, but sometimes looking before him, for fear he might trip on some stone or make a false step, and sometimes at the vessel he is carrying, for fear it might lean on one side." You must act in the same manner when leaving meditation.

299. This is the reason why we ask of God and the Blessed Virgin, in a formal manner, to defend and protect us against the enemies who are about to assail us with a rage so much the greater as we are more firmly resolved to remain faithful. We remind Jesus, our Savior, that he came upon earth to inflame our hearts with the fire of love that burns in his own heart. We do not grow tired asking for the intercession of the most holy Virgin Mary, of St. Joseph, and in their person, that of all our holy patrons, that the hopes, designs, and promises of Jesus Christ may be fully accomplished in us. For us,

indeed, nothing is comparable to the Will of God, always just, always wise, always amiable! To make it reign everywhere, and principally in our hearts will be the object of our efforts, our happiness and glory, as well as the last word of our meditation. No other disposition would be better able to close the audience, mark the fruit of meditation, and procure the glory of God the Father, Son, and Holy Ghost, to which none has contributed more than the Immaculate Virgin Mary.

300. These various thoughts are comprised in the following prayers which constitute the ordinary termination of our meditations:

PRAYER. Defend, we beseech thee, O Lord, by the intercession of the blessed Mary ever Virgin, this thy family from all adversity; and mercifully protect us, now prostrate before thee with our whole hearts from all the snares of our enemies. Through Christ our Lord. Amen. O Heart of Jesus burning with love for us. Inflame our hearts with love for thee. Pray for us, O Holy Mother of God. That we may be made worthy of the promises of Christ. Pray for us, O Holy Father Joseph. That we may be made worthy of the promises of Christ. The most just, most high, and most amiable will of God be done, praised, and eternally exalted in all things. May the Father, Son, and Holy Ghost be glorified in all places by the Immaculate Virgin Mary.

OREMUS. Defende, quaesumus, Domine, beata Maria semper Virgine intercedente, istam ab omni adversitate familiam, et totum corde tibi prostratam ab hostium insidiis propitius tuere clementer insidiis. Per Christum Dominum nostrum. Amen. Cor Jesu, flagrans amore nostri, inflamma cor nostrum amore tui. Ora pro nobis, sancta Dei Genitrix; ut digni efficiamur promissionibus Christi. Ora pro nobis, sancte Pater Joseph; ut digni efficiamur promissionibus Christi. Fiat, laudetur atque in æternum superexaltetur justissima, altissima et amabilissima voluntas Dei in omnibus. Pater et Filius et Spiritus Sanctus ubique glorificentur per Immaculatam Virginem Mariam!

14

HOW TO PROCEED, WHEN THE SUBJECT OF THE MEDITATION IS A FACT, INSTEAD OF BEING A TRUTH

301. In the foregoing explanations, we have habitually supposed the subject of meditation to be a moral truth. But the directions we have given apply as well to meditation when the subject is a fact, for example, an action or an entire event in the life of our Lord, of the Blessed Virgin, or the saints, or a mystery of our holy religion; or when the subject is a mixed one, i.e., when it comprises at once truth and a fact, such as death, judgment, etc.

302. This last case is the most frequent one, since, according to a remark of St. Augustine, all the actions in the life of our Savior, and let us add, in the history of the Church, teach a lesson, just as the words teach a fact. On this account, in most of the meditations, the truths are connected with facts, and the facts always contain an instruction; hence it follows that the considerations are suggested by the examination of facts as well as by the study of truths.

303. The process is therefore always the same; it would then not be necessary, it would hardly be useful, to add here some remarks. Thus you will perceive, during the course of the meditation, when and at what parts, it is proper and natural to have recourse to what is called the *application of the senses*, especially of the sight and hearing. With the imagination, figure yourself beholding the scene, the place,

the persons; listening to their words, to their discourse; assisting at what they do, or suffer, etc. Then put questions, and study the circumstances as if it concerned a truth, following the method already traced out. In this manner the facts give rise to thoughts, reflections, examinations in order to know better what we are or ought to be; these are precisely the *considerations*.

304. As to the other parts, the *affections*, the *resolutions*, and the *conclusion*, they are identical. There is therefore no reason to delay any longer in tracing such shades as are scarcely noticeable in theory by an acute observer, but whose distinction is without application in practice.

15

HOW TO PROCEED IN THE EXERCISE CALLED MIXED MENTAL PRAYER

305. The *mixed* mental prayer is, as its name implies, at once *oral* and *mental* prayer. It may be considered as a reading or vocal prayer interrupted for a lesser or greater length of time by mental prayer, or as a mental prayer drawing its inspiration more or less from a book or text of vocal prayer.

306. The subject of mental prayer is chosen either from a book; as, the Holy Scriptures, especially the psalms and the Gospel, the Imitation of Jesus Christ, the Spiritual Combat, the Constitutions, the Circulars, the book of Spiritual reading, the book of meditations, etc.; or from some formula of vocal prayer; as, the *Pater, Ave, Gloria Patri, Litanies*, etc. St. Francis of Assisi recited the Lord's prayer with particular devotion, pondering on the words, and meditating on the sense they contained; he even composed a paraphrase on it. The versicle *Gloria Patri* made likewise a most lively impression on his soul, and formed one of his fervent aspirations; he repeated it frequently and counseled it to others. A lay-brother, who was much tempted to devote himself to study, came to ask his permission for that purpose, "My dear Brother," the saint said to him, "learn the *Gloria Patri*, often repeat this doxology, and you will become wise in the sight of God." The Brother obeyed; and, in a short time, he made rapid progress in

the spiritual life, and was no longer tempted to study. Lastly, the ordinary prayers of the Christian and religious, morning and night prayers, the office, the prayers which precede or follow the exercises, etc., may furnish excellent texts for mixed mental prayer; at the same time, the meditation on these subjects will singularly help us to recite these daily vocal prayers with devotion, and not through mere routine.

307. The thoughts and facts furnished by those formulas which are known by heart, or which we read from a book, constitute the subjects of meditation. Read or recite a first thought; if necessary, repeat it in order to understand it better; then stop and make the ordinary acts: the *considerations, affections,* and *resolutions,* according to the method above indicated. The processes are absolutely the same.

308. Then you will pass on to a second, third thought, and so on; i.e. read or recite that which furnishes matter for a second, a third thought. Pause whenever you feel yourself moved, and as long as the attention of your mind and the attraction of grace usefully retain you thereat.

309. Under this form, "meditation is like him that inhales the odor of the pink, rose, rosemary, thyme, jessamine, orange flower, distinctly one after another. Make use of a book, when your mind becomes tired; i.e. read a little, and then meditate, read again a little and then meditate, and continue thus until the end of your half hour. Mother Teresa made use of this process in the beginning, and said that she found it very good. I too have tried it, and derived much benefit from it." (St. Francis de Sales.)

310. We cannot err in following St. Teresa and St. Francis de Sales. Listen again to another distinguished master, St. Alphonsus of Liguori: "Whenever mental prayer is made in private, it is always good to make use of a meditation book. (This saint explains elsewhere that, by meditation book, he means pious books, such as the Lives of the Saints, the Way of Salvation, etc.) Pause at the most moving passages, without endeavoring to read the whole meditation. St. Francis de Sales says that in this we must imitate the bees, which

keep to one flower as long as they find any honey to be extracted, and then wing their flight to another. St. Teresa followed this method for seventeen years; she used to read a little, then meditated for some time." St. Philip Neri also told beginners to make use of a pious book, especially the Lives of saints; but he added that one ought not to read out of curiosity and eagerness but stop at each thought.

311. In the mixed mental prayer, there is a danger, against which it is necessary to be forewarned, because we are naturally drawn thereto: we must take care that mental prayer does not change into a continuous vocal prayer, or into a mere spiritual reading, or a religious study, or even a reading of pious curiosity; we would thus deprive ourselves of the advantages of mental prayer.

312. Spiritual reading possesses much affinity with mental prayer, especially if made with reflection; both constitute an interview with God. But, according to the remark of St. Augustine, "when we read, God speaks to us; when we pray, we speak to God. *Oratio est locutio ad Deum; quando enim legis, tibi loquitur Deus: quando oras, cum Deo loqueris.*" Spiritual reading is not mental prayer itself, but a substantial element of this exercise; because it furnishes pious thoughts, produces holy affections, and suggests good resolutions.

313. This truth is, to a greater extent, applicable to the mixed mental prayer; reading and prayer combined so as to keep up our attention, without, however, proving an obstacle to that interior and personal labor, which is the basis of every mental prayer.

16

HOW MENTAL PRAYER MAY BE COMBINED WITH OTHER EXERCISES OF PIETY

314. "The method teaches how mental prayer, animated by faith, can advantageously be reconciled with other exercises, such as the benediction of the blessed Sacrament, an instruction, the Way of the Cross, etc. Mental prayer is not replaced by these exercises; it is merely practiced in a peculiar form." (Const. S. M.) After the explanations contained in this Guide, you will hardly be embarrassed in the practice of meditation under any of these special forms. It will suffice to say in a few words what each one would do of his own accord, without any new indication, by following in all simplicity the way and the rules we have just traced out.

315. Before these exercises, which are to serve you for your mental prayer, make, at least in substance and very briefly, the acts which regularly precede every mental prayer, and constitute its preparation and introduction. Say these prayers as far as circumstances will permit. Often you can dispose of but very short moments; yet these acts may be restricted as well as extended: if you can dispose of one minute, do so, and God will bless this mark of good will.

316. During the exercise itself, whatever it may be, act as much as possible as in the mixed meditation; frequently you will find it useful to call on faith and to multiply your acts of faith. With reference to

what you will see, hear, and remark, it will be easy for you to draw from yourself some acts which may constitute the considerations, affections, and resolutions. The essential thing is that these acts emanate from yourself and be the spontaneous expression of what your soul thinks, feels, and desires. Under these circumstances, mental prayer may become remarkable for the fruit it bears and by the ease which distinguishes it from every other kind of meditation.

317. Furthermore, let us develop these indications, by taking as examples the exercises mentioned above (art. 314), because they are of the number which most easily combine with mental prayer. Is there an exercise more proper to facilitate the feeling of the presence of God, the expression of our homage, the account of our necessities and requests, the intimate and prolonged interview with our Lord, and this with greater ease, than the benediction with the Blessed Sacrament, where our Lord leaves his retirement to place himself at our disposal under visible appearances? It is a most solemn audience, to which we are admitted, where he reserves for us the most signal favors. Now the acts of faith, as well as the complementary acts, are imposed, as it were, when you find yourself in the presence of this august Sacrament, which the Church calls the mystery of faith, *mysterium fidei.*

318. The colloquy will be preferably held with the adorable person of our sweet Savior. You may choose the subject according to the rules of the method, or you may adhere to the mixed meditation by taking part in the chant and liturgical prayers. You will likewise find very appropriate subjects in the Office of the Blessed Sacrament, in the fourth book of the *Imitation of Jesus Christ,* in the Visits and other opuscules of St. Alphonsus Liguori, in the Litany of the Holy Name of Jesus.

319. Every visit to the Most Blessed Sacrament is, in its object and end, a divine audience, and consequently, a mental prayer, whatever be the duration or frequency of these visits. To present ourselves before God, without rendering him the homage due to his infinite majesty, would be an indignity; now the acts of this homage consti-tute a true mental prayer; they comprise at least an act of adoration

and of petition, which may be thus expressed: "My Jesus, present upon this altar, I adore thee with the angels who surround thy throne; bless me before I retire, to go whither duty calls me." If the visit be prolonged, diverse acts are made, according to the directions given in art. 135 and seq. A book or formula may be used, or we may seek inspirations from the circumstances of the moment, according to the necessities of our soul; but especially should we multiply the petitions, recalling to mind some texts of the Gospel, whether spoken by our divine Master, or only addressed to him: "*Magister adest, et vocat te;* the Master is here, and calls thee." (St. John XI, 28.) "*Ego vobiscum sum omnibus diebus usque ad consummationem saeculi;* I am with you all days, even to the consummation of the world." (Matt. XXVIII, 20.) "*Venite ad me omnes qui laboratis et onerati estis, et ego reficiam vos;* come to me all you that labor, and are heavy laden, and I will refresh you." (Matt. XI. 28.) "*Non est opus valentibus medicus, sed male habentibus;* they that are in health need not a physician, but they that are sick." (Matt. IX, 12.) "*Domine, ecce quem infirmatur;* Lord, behold he whom thou lovest is sick." (St. John XI, 3.) "*Infirmitas hæc non est ad mortem;* this sickness is not unto death." (St. John XI, 4.)

320. Is there an exercise which speaks more eloquently to our soul, which moves more vividly her deepest recesses, which more completely employs all her faculties, than the exercise of the Way of the Cross? Where could you find a richer source of pious considerations, a more ardent furnace for holy affections, lastly, stronger motives for suggesting and strengthening the best resolutions? There you have a resume of the greatest truths of our holy religion, a representation of the most stirring events, and the most eloquent example of all virtues. It is therefore not surprising to learn that the Passion of our Lord is the subject most universally chosen for meditation, and the one most highly esteemed by the saints.

321. To sustain the attention, you may sometimes make use of a book, but do not neglect to make your own considerations. When the exercise of the Way of the Cross is done in community, the reading of the considerations becomes necessary; but this reading should be done slowly, that the affections may find time to develop themselves.

It is also proper to prepare the soul for these meditations by procuring from time to time the food of a spiritual reading on the Passion of our Lord.

322. The method pointed out in art. 189, which consists of asking a series of questions: Who has suffered? What has he suffered? For whom? Why? How, etc., produces excellent results in the considerations of the Way of the Cross.

323. Where are we placed in a better condition to converse with Almighty God, than in a reunion, where God speaks to us through the mouth of one of his ministers or representatives? Is it not enough to recall to mind what faith teaches about the excellence of the word of God, in order to listen attentively, to produce acts of adherence to what is said to us, to apply it to ourselves, to multiply with rapidity, even during the course of the instruction, acts of petition, thanks, and humility?

324. There exists no exercise of piety more easily transformed into a fervent mental prayer than Holy Mass. This holy sacrifice is, by nature, the solemn prayer, the liturgical act par excellence. It becomes the best meditation for each of us in particular, provided we assist thereat with lively faith.

325. What is holy Mass? It is, according to Faith, Jesus Christ himself, who prays on our altars, "*semper vivens ad interpellandum pro nobis;* always living to make intercession for us." (Hebr. VII, 25). He is our suppliant with his Father; he offered his life, death, body, and blood for us. With his prayer, he unites the prayer of the celebrant, as well as the prayers of those who assist at the Sacrifice. There is, in truth, but one priest, but one sacrificer, and, consequently, but one prayer. Thus, our Lord makes as his own our prayers, intentions, petitions, invocations, in a word, all our acts of mental prayer produced during Mass.

326. Never does our Savior find our petitions too great or too numerous, as we cannot ask for more than he has already given us, since he has given himself to us in Holy Mass. But he rectifies our petitions, cleanses them from their imperfections, and covers them

with his merits, so that they may be surely heard; "for thou hearest me always, *semper me audis.*" (St. John XI, 42).

327. What wonderful things we shall discover in this adorable sacrifice, when the veils which cover it, and make it a mystery of faith, *mysterium fidei,* shall have fallen! Already at present, we can catch sight of these wonders in a more abundant light in proportion as we consider them more attentively by the light of faith, i.e. by the prayer of faith. How this prayer of faith will be powerful in giving rise to affections, producing admiration and gratitude, and leading us to the prayer of supplication and of union with God! Even the prayers of the Missal and especially those of the canon of the Mass contain incomparable supplications. Try to take them sometimes as subjects of mixed mental prayer.

328. But the incomparable prayer, the prayer unique of this kind, is the prayer which is joined with Holy Communion. If there is on earth a meeting of man with God, a divine audience, where could it be found more complete than in Holy Communion? Could we even desire or imagine a more propitious occasion, more favorable time for mental prayer, than those moments which precede and those which follow Holy Communion? Who would dare to approach the holy Table, without, at the same time, making a mental prayer, i.e. without reflecting piously about this act? God gives himself to the soul, the soul receives her God: behold a spectacle worthy of the admiration of the Angels. We ought to fall into delightful raptures at the view of this ineffable condescension of God, if we had faith like a mustard seed. Let us, therefore, interrogate faith; let us meditate on the answers given by faith to the questions enumerated in art. 207. Who is coming to me? To whom is he coming? Why? How? What must I do? How must I receive him? What shall I ask? What shall I promise? What shall I expect?

329. Conformably to preceding recommendations, entertain yourself first with the most holy Virgin, with the angels and saints, who should assist you in the preparation and thanksgiving. Then address yourself to our Lord (art. 240 and seq.); speak to him, he is there, he is before you, he is within you, he is but one with you. If you make use

of a book for the acts before and after Holy Communion, read slowly, and make of the reading a mixed mental prayer.

330. Just as the preparatory acts are of great importance in this kind of mental prayer, so too, you would deprive yourself of the greatest advantages of this exercise, if you were to neglect the acts of the conclusion. By these last, you supply what is wanting in the considerations, affections, and resolutions which you had not the time to produce properly during the course of the exercise, and thus secure to yourself the fruits you are to derive therefrom. Besides, no excuse could be admitted here: nothing can prevent you from finding a few minutes to make these acts, if not immediately after the instruction or other exercise, whatever it may be, at least in the course of the day.

17

HOW AND WHY THE EXAMINATION
OF MENTAL PRAYER IS MADE

331. Souls that take their progress in mental prayer to heart do not fail
to make regularly their daily examination of this exercise. This examination is, in some way, an integral part of mental prayer, as the proof
of a scientific solution is a part of the operation, if one wishes to be
sure whether it is correct or faulty.

332. It may be affirmed that it is impossible to make the daily
examination of mental prayer without becoming men of mental
prayer; nay, it is the shortest way for arriving at this end.

333. It is necessary to fix a time for this examination, for example,
several minutes of the time devoted to the particular examination.

334. As mental prayer is made under the protection of the
guardian angel, it is advisable to beg our guardian angel to assist us in
this complementary work.

335. The examination comprises all the parts of mental prayer, the
ensemble and the details; but for one day, or for one week, lay special
stress on such acts, or on this point, then on another.

336. Never omit to question yourself on the various preparations;
and in order to guide you in the discovery of your faults, peruse what
we have already said on this point. Observe the same for the consid-

erations, affections, and resolutions. Never fail to examine yourself on the special or principal resolution.

337. Nothing is more useful than to direct your attention to the ordinary defect of your mental prayer, as well as to the special defect of your last meditation, so that you may avoid it next time.

338. We recommend the infliction of penance for the ensemble of the faults ascertained, and for every fault grievous in itself, in its consequences, or circumstances. One profitable penance would consist in resuming every meditation, in which there has been too much negligence; for this, we should choose the first leisure moments. Experience proves that this remedy is very efficacious, although the new meditation were to last but five minutes.

339. Another excellent means to aid us in making our meditation well, is to keep an account of it in writing, with a personal estimate of the exercise. This account should be short; not to make it brief, would be exposing ourselves often to forget it, and soon to neglect it altogether. It will be a great assurance to you that you will persevere in this practice, if you submit your account to your director. It is likewise advantageous to enter into a memorandum-book, immediately after meditation, the thoughts, sentiments, and resolutions which have made an impression on you; by putting them in writing, we come to understand and retain them better. In after-life, these notes are perused with great profit and even with pleasure: the soul experiences that which we feel when meeting again with old acquaintances.

340. We here give a summary of the most ordinary questions in the examination of mental prayer; each one will modify the questions, according as it concerns the daily or monthly examination. In the monthly examination, we endeavor to know our habitual dispositions rather than our faults; in this, it differs from the daily examination. To arrive at a satisfactory result, it is not necessary to examine ourselves thoroughly on each of these questions if time does not allow; it suffices to dwell more seriously, sometimes on one, sometimes on another of these points. The essential thing is to make a brief examination each day and a complete one each month.

341. Here follow the points on which it is useful to question ourselves:

1. Have I advanced or retrograded in what concerns the *remote preparation:* control over myself and my passions, struggle against sin, against every irregular allurement: dissipation, carelessness, pride, sensuality, silence, recollection, vigilance, remembrance of the presence of God, practice of ejaculatory prayers, and esteem for mental prayer?

2. How do I perform the *proximate preparation:* choice of subject and fruit to be derived therefrom, exactness, and respectful bearing?

3. How do I habitually make the various acts of the *immediate preparation:* invocation of the Holy Ghost, representation of the subject, recommendation to the guardian angel, recourse to the most holy Virgin, to St. Joseph, and to my holy Patrons; acts of faith in the presence of God, and other complementary acts of faith?

4. Have I endeavored to make the *prayer of faith* by repeated acts of faith in the presence and word of God, by interrogating and listening to Faith, i.e. to God, to his doctrine, to his Gospel, to his Church, to his saints, to my rules, in order to conform my thoughts, judgments, words, and actions to them?

5. Have I applied myself to the *prayer of meditation* or *considerations* by endeavoring to penetrate myself with the lessons conveyed by the truth, or the fact on which I am meditating? Have these considerations produced a salutary impression on my soul?

6. Have I applied myself to the *prayer* of *supplication* or *affections*, especially to the invocations suggested by the meditation on the subject or by the needs of my soul?

7. Have I applied myself to the *prayer* of *union* of *conformity* to the will of God, by taking resolutions calculated to conduct my soul to such dispositions and to strengthen her therein? Have I taken an efficacious resolution to gain a decisive victory over a special fault, or to advance in a particular virtue? Have I renewed it in every meditation, until success was complete, or at least satisfactory? How far am I in this work? Why have I not kept my resolutions? What must I do to remove the cause of these faults?

8. Which is the saddest defect of my last meditation, and which are the *principal* or the *ordinary difficulties* during my meditations? What is the cause thereof, and what have I to do to remove this cause forever?

9. Do I, during meditation, endeavor to awaken in myself, and keep up sentiments of *humility* and *confidence* in preference to all other sentiments? Impressed with these sentiments, do I apply myself to increase the acts of humility and the invocations, whenever I am reduced to powerlessness, or have difficulties to encounter?

10. How do I habitually make the acts of the *conclusion*, and how do I spend the first moments after mental prayer?

11. Am I convinced that the time of mental prayer is the time *most usefully employed,* even for succeeding in the functions of my charge and for promoting the true interests of the works and of the persons entrusted to my responsibility?

12. I must at any cost become a man of meditation! Am I well convinced that such is the will of God in my regard? Do I really believe that meditation is an *easy exercise,* not beyond my capacity, that I can and ought to succeed in it? To what must I, in consequence, apply myself during the coming month, or in my next meditation?

13. How is it that, after so many months and years, I am still so far from being a man of meditation? Why am I so easily induced to perform mental prayer *with negligence,* to lose so many and such precious moments during this holy exercise, and to languish thus, perhaps, until death?

14. Against *what defect* or towards what point must I direct my principal efforts? What does God require of me, that I may become, with his grace, a man of prayer?

WHY GOD PERMITS US TO ENCOUNTER DIFFICULTIES DURING MENTAL PRAYER. WHICH ARE THE ORDINARY DIFFICULTIES AND HOW WE CAN TRIUMPH OVER THEM

342. A true guide is not satisfied with showing the way: he forewarns the traveler against dangers, strengthens him against obstacles and fatigues, and defends him against enemies; in short, he tries to make the route sure and easy. Our work would be incomplete, were we not to speak of the dangers encountered on the way; we could even be accused of inaccuracy, because we have so often affirmed that the road is sure and easy, and that it suffices for each one to will, in order to arrive infallibly at the term, i.e. to become a man of prayer.

343. Well then, let us boldly affirm, mental prayer has its difficulties and fatigues, not only like every physical, moral and intellectual labor, but also, and especially, because it is the source of the greatest blessings. The enemy of God, who is also our enemy, knows it, and he does not forget it; he omits nothing that can prevent us from becoming men of prayer.

344. "The demon knows, that when the soul applies herself to mental prayer with perseverance, she is lost for him," says St. Teresa. He profits, therefore, without ever being discouraged, of the permission given him by God to tempt us; he has an implacable hatred against the man of meditation, as he had against Job. It is especially during meditation that he is going about us, like a roaring lion, trying

at least to prevent us from prayer: "*Adversarius vester diabolus, tamquam leo rugiens, circuit quærens quem devoret.*" (I Peter V, 8.)

345. He is on the lookout, he knows from which side he can attack us most securely: fickleness of our spirit and imagination, subjection to the senses, allurements of the heart, weakness of the will, discouragement caused by want of success. He takes advantage of everything so that mental prayer may bear no fruit, and finally, we may become disgusted with it.

346. It is with the difficulties in mental prayer like with every other temptation; they are unavoidable but useful. "*Fili, accedens ad servitutem Dei, sta in justitia, et timore et præpara animam tuam ad tentationem.* Son, when thou comest to the service of God, stand in justice and fear, and prepare thy soul for temptation." (Ecclus. II, 1.) "*Qui non est tentatus, quid scit?* What doth he know, that hath not been tried?" (Ecclus. XXXIV, 9.) "*Quia acceptus eras Deo, necesse fuit ut tentatio probaret te;* because thou wast acceptable to God, it was necessary that temptation should prove thee." (Tobias XII, 13.) What is said of Tobias is also said of Abraham, the patriarchs, the apostles, and, in general, of all the saints.

347. Distractions, dryness, and other difficulties which we encounter in meditation, are useful and even necessary to maintain us in humility, to ensure our progress, to prevent us from falling, and to preserve the merits we have already acquired. "It is in dryness that we profit most," says St. Alphonsus Liguori.

348. Let us enter into some details. Obstacles in prayer are ordinarily classified under three heads: *distractions, dryness,* and *illusions.* Some of the remedies used against these evils are specific for one of these maladies; most of them are, however, efficacious against all three.

349. We call distraction every inattention of the soul to the subject which ought to occupy her; as the word indicates it, the *distracted* soul is *drawn* far from the subject with which she wished or ought to busy herself.

350. All distractions may be classified in two categories: those that are voluntary, and those that are involuntary. We need not give

ourselves any pains about the involuntary distractions, because they do not render us culpable, nor are they injurious, as long as they remain involuntary. Now, they are involuntary as long as we are not aware of them. As soon as they are perceived, we must combat them as voluntary distractions.

351. Distractions may be voluntary in different ways and degrees: in themselves and their causes, on account of the negligence in banishing them, etc.

352. One thing is always in your power; it is to commence well, i.e. to think of what you are going to do. At the beginning of each action, you must take care to direct your intention. If you proceed thus in your mental prayer, says St. Thomas, you will assure to yourself the principal fruits of every well-made prayer. If, besides, you are careful to keep yourself in the presence of God, by doing nothing that recalls your first intention, you remain, in consequence of a virtual intention, under the salutary influence of grace; God communicates himself to you, and like a wholesome nourishment, he penetrates and endows you with supernatural strength.

353. The general cause of our distractions is levity, inconstancy, restlessness, in a word, dissipation of the mind. Attention was already called to this fault in the remote preparation treated of in art. 98; it is so serious, however, that we judge it useful again to insist on the fact that it is impossible to change a dissipated man into a man of meditation. A dissipated man is compared to a fortress whose keepers amuse themselves, and are diverted from their duty by every object that presents itself. Thus the dissipated soul is open to all comers, she is enticed successively to the right and to the left, to a distance, to every side, by the impression of the senses, by the wanderings of the imagination, by the passions of the heart, by seductions of every kind; she no longer belongs to herself, she has no control over her faculties.

354. How could she be able, under such circumstances, to recollect herself in order to converse with God, to make mental prayer? Can she even know what she desires, whither she is going, what she is doing? Can she stop at the considerations which would throw some light upon her state? In the parable of the sower, the dissipated soul is

compared to a highway; the seed which falls thereon remains on the surface and is immediately carried away or trodden under foot; it cannot even begin to take root. None can therefore accuse of exaggeration those who affirm that dissipation is frequently more dangerous than sin itself. In reality, the sinner can enter into himself, the dissipated man cannot, he is powerless for meditation, and remains a prey to the most dangerous illusions. If you discover in yourself this serious malady, have recourse, from this very day, to the remedies which ought to effect the cure.

355. In order to root out this evil, we must attack the causes that produce it. We will just enumerate the ordinary causes, leaving to each one the care of combating those from which he suffers. Natural predisposition, freedom of the imagination, predominating empire of the senses, an indifference which does not take the trouble to govern itself, the habit of treating everything with lightness, of being continually absent-minded, of giving oneself to everybody and everything, that eagerness for affairs which do not concern us, even the ill-regulated desires for the holiest works of supererogation; then the immoderate attachment to some occupation, too tender an affection for creatures, the curiosity that wants to see, visit, hear, know, read everything: books, newspapers, reviews, novels; lastly, and particularly, intemperance of speech: behold what produces, keeps up, and develops dissipation, a fault as incompatible with mental prayer as motion is irreconcilable with rest.

356. Commence the warfare, be pitiless towards yourself; do not cease to struggle until you are completely victorious; and if you will believe me, direct your first efforts against your habitual infractions of silence; for, without silence, there is no recollection, and without recollection, no mental prayer.

357. It is evident that he who does not struggle against these causes will never meditate well; it is also evident that he who is faithful to the rules of preparation thereby removes all these causes. As we have already said, the chief, if not the only cause why there are so few men of prayer, is the want of preparation. Look therefore on the preparation as an integral part of meditation. Is it not what the

Holy Spirit wished to communicate, in addressing to us this recommendation: "*Ante orationem præpara animam;* before prayer prepare thy soul." (Ecclus. XVIII, 23.)

358. In removing the causes, the preparation takes away most of the distractions; but it does not remove all of them, because as, after Cassian, St. Alphonsus Liguori says, "it is impossible for our mind to apply itself to meditation without having any distractions."

359. We are not answerable for these distractions until we are aware of them; but it is then also that they can be disavowed by our mind, repelled by our heart, and combated by our will.

360. The battle is changed immediately into victory, if you have recourse to an act of faith in the presence of God, followed by acts of humility, of supplication, or by ejaculatory prayers.

361. If all the time were employed in these acts, mental prayer would not be defective; but as soon as you feel yourself in the normal state, take up the subject where the distraction made you lose sight of it. And if renewed distractions oblige you thus to come back on yourself five, ten, twenty times, do not become impatient on that account; return twenty times to the same acts, and you will make great progress in meditation. This is the prayer of patience, of which St. Francis de Sales spoke thus to one of his religious daughters: "Never, my child, have you made such a good prayer."

362. Listen again to the sweet St. Francis de Sales on the same subject: "If you are troubled with distractions, make the prayer of patience and humility. Beseech Almighty God to be your support, to give you a desire to love him, to pray to him, and other similar things. When your heart wanders or is distracted, lead it gently back to its point, place it back tenderly near its Master. If you were to do nothing else during the whole time than very graciously taking your heart back and placing it near our Lord, although it would wander as many times as you had led it back, the time would be well employed, and you would perform an exercise very agreeable to your dear Spouse."

363. You may also have recourse to some exterior means: look at the crucifix, the tabernacle, at an image of the most holy Virgin; take a book, say some vocal prayers, repeat some ejaculatory prayers. But

proceed always gently, do not get into a passion, and do not lose confidence. *Cui resistite in fide;* withstand the enemy with a confidence inspired by faith. "*In omnibus sumentes scutum fidei, in quo possitis omnia tela nequissimi ignea exstinguere;* in all things take the shield of faith, wherewith you may be able to extinguish all the fiery darts of the most wicked one." (Eph. VI, 16.) Yes, trust in God, in his goodness, his power, his promises, and his designs upon you. He wants you to become a man of prayer, therefore you will be it. In God's mind, the difficulties which he permits are *in your favor*, and not *against* you.

364. Therefore, I beseech you, never to lay down your arms, never to lose courage, either to let the distractions take possession of the ground in all freedom or to abandon the exercise of mental prayer. Nothing is more offensive to God and more detrimental to the soul than discouragement; it is, towards God, a lack of faith and confidence, a defect to which the Divine Master attributes the want of success in our prayers; on our part, it shows a want of humility, at least, a commencement of pride. To abandon mental prayer for such motives is to throw ourselves into the arms of our mortal enemy. Thus, never give way to discouragement; in any condition, the prayer of faith, of the presence of God, and of supplication by means of ejaculatory prayers is easy. (See art. 248.) Only the demons and the damned lie under an impossibility of praying, for if they could pray, they would be saved.

365. It happens sometimes that the soul resembles a dry and arid desert bearing no fruit, giving no sign of life and vegetation; there exists a complete barrenness. We call *dryness* or aridity that state of the soul, in which she finds herself sterile or unable to produce the acts of mental prayer. Between absolute sterility and the mere difficulty of performing all the acts of mental prayer in a proper manner, there are very many degrees.

366. What has been said of distractions may be said of the state of dryness; it is either voluntary or involuntary. Voluntary dryness should, like voluntary distractions, be combated above all in its cause, by fidelity to the remote preparation. Pride, egotism, sensuality, want of simplicity in obedience, cunning, worldly policy in our way of

acting, are frequent causes of aridity in mental prayer. "You will not be simple and artless as a little child, you shall therefore not get the sweetmeats of a little child." (St. Francis de Sales.)

367. Then the state of sterility should be combated by a direct struggle during the meditation itself; i.e. by acts of faith in the presence and other attributes of God, but especially by acts of humility, confidence, and supplication (art. 235 and seq.). Even if these acts should not seem to us to come from the heart, but to be restricted to a mere movement of the lips and mouth, they would suffice for us to constitute a state of prayer. If it grieves us to be in such a state, we make, according to St. Augustine, an excellent prayer: "*quia si vel hoc dolemus jam oremus.*"

368. Besides, the state of dryness is frequently prolonged without any fault of ours; here, as in the physical order, it is not in our power to produce rain for the refreshment of the soil whenever we wish. We must then be resigned, for it is a most painful trial, and yet experience proves that God does not exempt his best friends and servants from it; proof thereof is St. Teresa, St. Ignatius, St. Francis de Sales, and St. Alphonsus Liguori. In such a state, mental prayer becomes an insupportable burden; nothing is felt in this exercise but weariness and disgust, and at times, violent temptations, darkness, and great discouragement.

369. Be on your guard, then, voluntarily to yield to distractions, and to abandon the exercise of mental prayer. Listen to St. Teresa: "Very often, I confess, I would have preferred the most severe penance to the torment of recollecting myself for meditation. I had a desperate struggle to sustain in going to the oratory, and on entering, I found myself seized with mortal sadness. Nevertheless, I made an effort to overcome myself, and God came to my help...."

370. "It is by aridities and temptations that the Lord tries those who love him. Even if this trial were to last during the entire life, a soul ought not to abandon mental prayer; a time will come when everything will be amply repaid. The love of God does not consist in experiencing tender affections, but in serving him with courage and humility." (St. Teresa.)

371. Behold a remedy counseled by St. Augustine: "We should be like the famished children of God; during mental prayer, let us ask for alms at the gates of his presence because he gives food to the hungry. *Famelici Dei esse debemus; ante januam conspectus illius in orationibus mendicemus; ipse dat escam esurientibus.*" "In moments of interior dryness and aridity of spirit," says St. Philip Neri, "it proves an excellent remedy to consider ourselves as mendicants in the presence of God and the saints, and thus to draw near, sometimes to one saint, sometimes to another, to ask him for spiritual alms, with the same earnestness and sincerity as poor people do, who hold out their hand to us." This is, under a striking form, the recourse to the prayer of faith, of the presence of God, and of supplication (arts. 235 and 236).

372. Finally, let us listen to the consoling and encouraging words of St. Alphonsus: "It is in dryness that we profit most. Then, let us be humble and resigned, when beholding ourselves without fervor, without desire, and almost unable to produce any act of virtue. Let us be humble, I say, and resigned: this meditation will be more profitable to us than the others. If in this case we can do nothing else, let us be content with saying: Help me, Lord, have mercy on me, and do not abandon me. Let us have recourse to Mary, our Mother and our comfort. Happy is he who in desolation remains faithful to the practice of mental prayer! God will shower down his graces upon him."

373. But for the seemingly abandoned soul, nothing equals the consolation conveyed by these words of St. Francis de Sales: "The more God deprives us of consolations, the more we should endeavor to testify our fidelity towards him. A single act made in dryness of spirit is worth more than many acts made with tenderness of spirit, because it is the fruit of stronger love... As a mother refuses sugar to her child which has the threadworm, so God takes consolations from us when we take a vain satisfaction in them and are subject to the worm of presumption... Let us patiently await the return of consolation, let us go on our way, let us not, on that account, omit any exercise of devotion, but if possible rather multiply our good works..."

374. "I nevertheless approve that you tell your affliction to your sweet Savior, but lovingly and without haste, because he is pleased

that we speak to him of the evils he has inflicted on us, and complain to him; but it should be with love and humility, and to himself, as little children do, when their mother has chastised them. Nevertheless, we must also suffer something and with sweetness."

375. Finally, let us be resigned to the holy will of God; it is always to this conclusion that we must come. Besides, has the object of mental prayer not been attained? Do you believe that your soul, kept in the presence of God, has not been nourished by substantial food, and strengthened in virtue? Are you not better able to fulfill your duties? Is not this the very end of mental prayer?

376. Whenever the demon does not succeed in diverting the soul from mental prayer by other attacks, he endeavors to draw her into illusions. As the effect of the remedies we have already indicated with regard to distractions and dryness is also to forewarn us against illusions, or to withdraw us from them if we had had the misfortune to become their prey, we have but to complete some of the indications already given in order to render the mind more attentive thereto.

377. A first illusion consists in believing that mental prayer is too difficult and that we shall never succeed in making it well. All that we have already said of the facility of meditation proves that this is a wrong idea; we will therefore not try to refute it.

378. We meet with souls that seem to have a good will, but they are convinced that it is useless for them any longer to try to make mental prayer, or to make it well, since they witness no result.

379. It is, first of all, to be remarked that mental prayer would not be useless, even were its results restricted to prevent us from falling or relapsing; but, practiced with a good will, mental prayer will always make us advance. Do not more endeavor to see your progress in virtue, than to see or hear the grass grow day after day. These developments are as difficult to ascertain in the moral as well as in the physical order; the work of progress proceeds slowly and insensibly. Mental prayer is a spiritual nourishment, whose effects we do not immediately perceive. "If the human heart exercises itself in meditation, it will always become more and more united to the divine Goodness, but by imperceptible advances, which are not very plainly

remarked while they are made, but when they are made." (St. Francis de Sales.)

380. Do not estimate the value of your meditations either by the consolations you experience, or by the weariness you suffer, or by the stationary condition you remark, but by the good will you feel after it, by the more marked esteem for the Rule, for obedience, for mortification, etc. In a good meditation, we do not learn to feel, but to will, not to be perfect, but to labor incessantly to become so.

381. "The resolutions," says St. Francis de Sales, "are the great fruits of mental prayer, which, without them, is very often not only useless, but even dangerous, because the virtues meditated upon but not practiced sometimes inflate the mind and courage, and cause us to think that we are such as we have resolved to be."

382. It is likewise an illusion if we believe to be something because we have made meditation with exactitude, with certain method, and even with pleasure; because we had, during meditation, some good thought, some pious velleity; because we have admired the beauty of virtue, and found vice detestable; because we have experienced disgust at the wickedness of the world, grieved over the lukewarmness and faults of the neighbor, conceived a thousand projects of zeal and formed thousands of desires for the greater glory of God. But we are not concerned about ourselves, except to say with the Pharisee, in a complete and very dangerous illusion: "O God, I thank thee that I am not like those living in the world, not even like such a one of my Brothers; I am attached to thee, I perform the exercises of a Christian and religious life, I even perform works of supererogation, etc."

383. According to the testimony of the saints, the following are some of the marks by which we may know that we are not subject to these illusions, and that mental prayer brings forth good fruit; it is, above all, an excellent sign, if we go out from meditation with the conviction that we must commence with the reform of ourselves, and that no reform is more necessary nor more pressing. After each meditation, says the author of the Imitation of Christ, "every day we ought to renew our purpose, and stir ourselves up to fervor, as if it were the first day of our conversion, and to say: Help me, Lord God, in my good

purpose, and in thy holy service, and grant that I may this day begin indeed, since what I have hitherto done is nothing." (Imit. I, 19.) He who does not keep, before all and constantly, at his own renovation, works under an illusion.

384. The reform of your interior conduct is explained by your exterior conduct, and especially by your behavior towards your neighbor. Make your meditations well, and you will find your charity becoming every day more and more real. True charity, you know, is patient, benevolent, and full of attention: it excuses all, explains all in good part, forgives all, is ingenious in cementing the union of hearts and minds. "Do you wish to know whether you have made meditation well? See whether your heart is filled with kind and charitable affections towards your neighbor." (St. Francis de Sales.)

385. "Interior renovation necessarily leads to a more unreserved abnegation of one's self, which is a third sign of a good mental prayer. Progress in the diverse spiritual exercises is estimated by the renunciation of our self-love, self-will, and of our ease." (St. Ignatius of Loyola.)

386. A fourth sign of a well-made mental prayer is a complete abandonment to the will of God; this is the very end of mental prayer. "The sovereign means for obtaining from God whatever we wish is, before all, to ask in our meditation, not for what we wish, but for what God wishes of us. God is more pleased with the least act of obedience and submission to his will in us than by all the services which we would propose to render him according to our own taste and inclination." (St. John of the Cross.)

387. Finally, the surest sign of the goodness of our mental prayer is our advancement in humility and obedience; in practice, these virtues are inseparable and are like the nourishing soil of the flowers and fruits of meditation. We love, therefore, to repeat in conclusion: apply yourself to meditation, and you will obtain the precious gift of humility; apply yourself to humility, and you will obtain the gift of meditation; these two virtues are never found one without the other. Be then humble, acknowledge your weakness, your impotence, your unworthiness, your nothingness; repel every vain satisfaction with

yourself, all self-love and egotism, and God will look down upon you with benevolence: "*Respexit humilitatem......Deposuit potentes de sede et exaltavit humiles*; He hath regarded the humility......He hath put down the mighty from their seat, and hath exalted the humble." (Luke I, 48, 52.) "*Deus superbis resistit, humilibus autem dat gratiam*; God resisteth the proud, and giveth grace to the humble." (James IV, 6.)

388. Be a little child by your humility, be also a little child by your confidence in your Father, by your filial abandonment; leave to God the choice of the kind of mental prayer best suited for you. There is the prayer of consolation and that of abandonment, the prayer of action and that of patience, the prayer of personal work and that of grace, the prayer of struggle and that of peace, etc. Which is the best for you? It is that which God reserves to you. As for you, go to meditation when duty or the Rule calls you thither; go there through obedience, with humility and confidence, but well prepared.

19

HOW WE OUGHT TO ENDEAVOR TO MAKE OUR MENTAL PRAYER A "PRAYER OF FAITH"

389. Although we have everywhere put in relief the role of faith, we think it useful to insist still on this point, since it is the distinctive character of mental prayer and of the method we recommend. "Mental prayer is all faith, it revolves upon the truths of faith, it is made by the light of faith, it establishes the soul in the light of faith; faith is its principle, its object and instrument." (Father Chaminade.)

390. "All the acts which enter into mental prayer are either directly or indirectly acts of faith, to such a point that we can say, faith only is necessary for meditation. The very conditions necessary for making meditation well are likewise based on faith." (Suarez.)

391. Faith is the basis or principle on which mental prayer and the practice of mental prayer rest; *"Fides fons orationis"* (St. Augustine). If you suppress faith, or the acts of faith in the existence, goodness, power, word, and promise of God, you render impossible, not only the practice, but even the idea of mental prayer. Without doubt, "it is hope and charity that pray; but faith believes, and since hope and charity cannot exist without faith, faith prays likewise." (St. Augustine.) This holy Doctor goes so far as to say: *"Non orat nisi fides;* it is faith alone that prays."

392. The more your faith in God, in all the infinite perfections of his being, will be lively and profound, the more meditation will become for you an easy, worthy, honorable, and advantageous exercise, the more lovingly and eagerly you will practice it. The gift of meditation is proportioned to that of faith, and the gift of faith increases with the petitions we make to God for this purpose. "*Fides fundit orationem, fusa oratio fidei impetrat firmitatem.* Faith diffuses prayer; but prayer, in its turn, confirms faith." (St. Augustine.) Therefore you should place amongst the most familiar of your ejaculatory prayers, the following: "*Adauge nobis fidem.* Increase our faith." (Luke XVII, 5.) "*Credo, Domine, adjuva incredulitatem meam.* I believe, Lord, come to the assistance of my want of faith." (Mark IX, 33.)

393. Faith is likewise the instrument of mental prayer, the means of becoming men of mental prayer, the road which leads to the perfect practice of mental prayer. Thus, first of all, it is by faith, that we approach God, for the special audience of meditation: "*Accedentem ad Deum, credere oportet quia est.* He that cometh to God must believe that he is." (Hebr. XI, 6.)

394. Faith is the light in which God manifests himself to our souls, the medium through which his words, his thoughts, the expression of his will come to us. Faith is therefore our habitual and ordinary means of communication with God.

395. Faith predisposes us for meditation by enlightening us about ourselves, about God, and about the relations which unite us with God. It reveals to us our principle, our end, our nature, our ignorance, our weakness, and our miseries, and then our sublime destiny; at the same time, it reveals to us all the wonders of God's goodness in our regard.

396. Finally, it represents to us mental prayer as the incomparable instrument, put into the hands of all, to obtain the entire accomplishment in our regard of all God's promises and designs.

397. Faith puts us in relation with the Divine Master, with his representatives, with Holy Church, and the saints; it places at our disposal the Gospel, the teachings of the Church and saints; it

procures for us the inestimable advantage of having the advice, the sentiment, the precept or counsel of our Lord, on every question, object, or whatever may interest our present conduct and our eternal future.

398. It is likewise from faith that we draw the desire, the will, the courage, the force, and the patience, with all the necessary dispositions in order to apply ourselves to meditation, and, despite all obstacles, to persevere in this holy exercise.

399. It is then by faith, that we commence, continue, and bring to the highest perfection the divine exercise of mental prayer.

400. It is, besides, by faith, and by the prayer of faith, that we take the habit of dwelling in the supernatural regions, that we converse familiarly with God, the Blessed Virgin, our guardian angel, and the saints, that we think as they do, that we have the same aspirations and the same will with them. In a word, our life is truly a life of faith: "*Justus autem meus ex fide vivit.*" (Hebr. X, 38.)

401. Thus, the prayer of faith is really the common source of all virtues, the practical school of perfection, and the direct road to our end.

402. We may still better account for the wonders operated by faith, if we try to measure the extent of the domain of faith, and if we are attentive to the fact that this domain is the same as that of meditation. Wherever faith penetrates, mental prayer follows, there to make choice of subjects for meditation, and of objects of affection.

403. The immense and even infinite domain of faith is summed up in the form of a table, in the Apostles' Creed, called in the Church, the symbol of faith, *symbolum fidei*. This formula is unique; nowhere, with no nation, at no epoch, will you find anything comparable to the symbol of our faith.

404. Taking this point of view, Rev. Father Chaminade found it therefore unnecessary to seek elsewhere for subjects of meditation. Whatever can be taken as a subject of meditation is implicitly contained in this symbol.

405. And first of all, we have said over and again how useful it is,

when considering the object of our faith, frequently to repeat this first word of the symbol: *Credo, I believe.* Retain and concentrate your attention on this affirmation, subjoining some questions like the following: Do I really believe? Am I convinced that God has revealed this truth to me? That his infallible authority proposes it to my belief? Do I believe with the certainty and the satisfaction of possessing the truth? I believe men of superior science in what they teach me; do I believe God, the infinite Wisdom and eternal Truth, more firmly than the man most worthy of belief? I believe, i.e. I am therefore as certain of the truths God deigns to reveal to me, as I am of the most evident and indubitable truths. If I believed more vividly, would not my life be in accordance with my faith? Would I not modify my judgments on this or that point?

406. What mysteries, what vivifying truths are accumulated in this beginning: *Credo in Deum* - I believe in God! To believe in the living and true God! How this faith elevates us above so many nations, which, for not possessing this belief in a true God, are plunged in the darkness of the grossest errors, and are seated in the shadows of death, i.e. of moral degradation. The more lively, full, and universal this belief in God of a Christian or of a people becomes, the more it elevates them, brings them nearer to God and to perfection. And it is the meditation of faith that operates these wonders.

407. Continue the recitation of the Creed: *Patrem omnipotentem Creatorem cœli et terrae.* As you pronounce these words, Faith gives you a glimpse of God, his nature and perfections, of the Trinity with its mysterious depths, the three adorable Persons, of the Creation, heaven, earth, the universe, the angels, man, of the history of angels and men, with God's plan for each part of the Creation.

408. Now we are at the second Person: *Et in Jesum Christum.* When St. Philip Neri, in his assiduous meditations on the symbol, came to these words, he was thrilled with joy and was rapt in the sweetest contemplations. What wonders do, indeed, unroll themselves before our eyes! The Incarnation of the Word, the Redemption of the human race, the incomparable figure of the most holy Virgin Mary, Mother of God, and Queen of the entire Creation; the life, apostolate,

and passion of our Lord, i.e. the most beautiful, sublime, and comprehensive subject of meditation! I insist on no point, I do not allow myself any comment, in order not to be drawn further than I would like.

409. To interrupt, I quote a simple reflection of St. Francis de Sales on the Passion: "I think," he says, "that Jesus Christ, besides the other objects he could have had in view, has wished to suffer many and diverse pains, such as the scourging, the crowning with thorns, the crucifixion, etc.; that having before our eyes all these sorrowful mysteries, we might have as many different subjects of meditation on the Passion, subjects from which we might draw various sentiments of gratitude and love."

410. According to St. Francis de Sales, St. Philip Neri, and others, the Passion of our Lord ought to be the ordinary subject of meditation for all Christians, because therein we may learn all things: the value of the soul, the malice of sin, the goodness and love of God, etc. How many volumes have not been written on these simple words: *passus sub Pontio Pilato, crucifixus, mortuus, et sepultus!*

411. I pass over immediately to an article which reveals to us, as it were, a new world, in the person and operations of the Holy Ghost; it is the supernatural world of grace, a thousand times more beautiful than the natural world, and more explicitly designated by the *Holy Catholic Church* and the *Communion of Saints;* here we find the mysteries of grace, the very end of Creation and Redemption, the family of God, the Divine Filiation, together with all the wonders it comprises, the sacraments, the Holy Eucharist, the remission of sins, the history of the Church and of the saints which comprises universal history and explains everything.

412. Finally, in these words: *credo vitam æternam,* you have the last end, the accomplishment of God's designs, and the crowning of his love; it is the eternity which will have no end, and will constitute our true life! There we shall see and contemplate face to face what faith shows us now as concealed with a veil.

413. In this compendium you have before you the history of all

that is. But what a compendium! What an ensemble and what details it unveils to us and permits us to divine!

414. Do you wish to take the Creed as the only and continual subject of your meditations? Behold how you are to proceed: after having placed yourself in the presence of God, says Rev. Father Chaminade, commence to recite the symbol with all the attention of which you are capable; then take up one article after another, consider each singly as long as you feel any attraction; pass on to the following article, as soon as distractions begin to turn you far from the subject. If any article makes no impression upon you, pass it without stopping, because there must be no contention of spirit; if you are able to keep your attention fixed only for one minute and feel the struggle would be useless to continue longer, do not try to keep it thereon two minutes. Go through the Creed, in this manner, perhaps two, three, or four times in a half-hour.

415. After some days, a change will be operated which will become apparent more and more; you will no longer succeed in going through in one half-hour all that one single article shall speak to your mind and heart. The considerations, and especially the affections, will come in crowds, you will stand before an inexhaustible mine, and soon you will discover that your life is too short to exhaust that which will be the object of your admiration for a whole eternity.

416. You will no longer stand in need of another book of meditations; you will possess all in the Creed. For all, whether in the order of nature or in that of grace, is implicitly comprised therein: the Trinity, Jesus Christ, Holy Church, Mary, the Gospel, the Apostles, the saints, finally all that is done in time, and will remain forever.

417. Thus the Creed is really the characteristic sign of the Christian, because outside of Christianity and of the symbol of faith, and of what is its commentary, you will nowhere find a collection of precise, exact, and satisfactory answers to all the questions which interest humanity.

418. The symbol reveals God and his work to us. What a book of meditations! It is the only one which explains all. This wonderful book unfolds before us the divine plan, and already presents to our

view the edifice which is constructed in time for eternity, on earth for heaven. Here below we see enough of the edifice to make out what it will be: the exterior and passing world forms its temporary portico, the Church prepares the living stones; we catch but a glimpse of what the crowning will be at the end of time.

20

HOW THE BLESSED VIRGIN IS THE PATRONESS AND MODEL OF MEN OF MENTAL PRAYER

419. Our counsels would be incomplete and our mission but imperfectly accomplished, were we not to add a few words to the relations existing between the Blessed Virgin and men of mental prayer. In truth, the Blessed Virgin Mary is the perfect model and the most powerful help we can propose to men of good will, who have resolved to devote themselves generously to the exercise of mental prayer.

420. When God distributed the most important parts and the highest functions in Holy Church, was not, in every thing, the best part reserved to the most blessed Virgin? No one would dare to affirm the contrary. Now, in the apostolic functions, this best part, according to the testimony of St. Peter and the apostles, is prayer: *"Nos vero orationi et ministerio verbi instanter erimus;* but we will give ourselves to prayer and the ministry of the word." (Acts VI, 4.)

421. Prayer, in its most sublime essence, is the occupation of the angels and saints in heaven; it will constitute their honor and joy during all eternity. Here below, prayer is likewise the highest, most heavenly, and most worthy of all occupations; it is, at the same time, the first instrument of the apostolate and the most powerful means of Christian zeal. On this account, prayer is placed before the preaching

of the word of God. For this same reason, the Divine Master employed thirty years in prayer and only three years in preaching; and yet during these three years, the greater part of the time was devoted to prayer. It was, therefore, the part of Mary, when cooperating in the salvation and redemption of the world, to pray, to live a life of prayer. She prayed in her infancy, in her family, in the temple; she prayed at Nazareth; she prayed while Jesus preached and immolated himself for us; she prayed on Calvary, she prayed in the Cenacle; she continued her ministry of prayer in the primitive church until her assumption into heaven.

422. The prayer of Mary possessed all the qualities we have pointed out: it was a prayer of faith and of the presence of God, then a prayer of meditation, of supplication, and of conformity to the will of God, or union with God.

423. Mary is the true model of the prayer of faith. Why have such great things been accomplished in her? Because her faith in all God has revealed was perfect. "*Beata quæ credidisti, quoniam perficientur ea quae dicta sunt tibi a Domino;* blessed art thou that hast believed, because those things shall be accomplished that were spoken to thee by the Lord." (Luke I, 45.)

424. The Gospel is very sparing in the details concerning the life of the most blessed Virgin, but each fact mentioned is a proof of her spirit of faith: The Annunciation, the Birth of Jesus, the flight into Egypt, the life at Nazareth, the apostolic life, the passion and death of Jesus, the first years of Holy Church, all are proof that the life of Mary could have been only a life of faith, and, as her prayer was continual, her life was likewise a continual prayer of faith.

425. Furthermore, we might say that her divine Son was pleased to exercise her in this life of faith by treating her in every circumstance according to rules that faith alone could find just and wise. Think only of the birth of Jesus in complete destitution, of the flight into Egypt, of the loss of Jesus in the temple, and of his answer to the loving complaint of his Mother. Think of the poor, laborious, and hidden life in the house of Nazareth, of the apostolic life of Jesus without apparent success, of the words of Jesus to his Mother at the

wedding of Cana, then of his last words on the Cross: "Woman, behold thy Son." Lastly, think of his death which seemed to terminate all without result. Is it thus that the Son of God should have come on earth, lived, and died? Faith alone could explain and sustain all, and faith was as vivid as unshaken in Mary. Hence, we salute her as *Virgo fidelis;* Virgin most faithful, pray for us, obtain for us the spirit and prayer of faith from thy Son, who is the Author of faith.

426. Whoever lived with God in more intimate, complete, and continual presence than the Blessed Virgin Mary? According to the most celebrated doctors, she enjoyed the clear vision of the blessed from the moment of her Immaculate Conception. When three years old, she went to the temple, in order to show still better that she remained unceasingly in the presence of God; from the moment of the Incarnation, she never separated from her Son and after the Ascension, she could only console herself by sighing after her dearly beloved Son. Who will reveal to us, especially, the mysteries of the hidden life of Nazareth? What was the principal occupation of Mary and Joseph? Was it not to contemplate Jesus, to admire him, to adore him, to give him thanks, then to work but for him, and to be at his service without reserve? Is not this a perfect and continual meditation? Has not St. Joseph been declared, on this account, the patron of the interior life and the model of divine prayer? What, then, should we say of Mary? Her life was a continual thought concentrated in God, i.e. an uninterrupted prayer, a prayer of faith and of the presence of God.

427. "*Maria autem conservabat omnia verba hæc conferens in corde suo.* Mary kept all these words, pondering them in her heart." (Luke II, 19.) The Holy Ghost himself gives her this testimony. Incessantly she revolved in her mind the unspeakable mysteries with which she was associated: the mystery of the incarnation, of the Redemption, of the Passion of her Son, etc. And as the Holy Ghost enlightened the soul of Mary with his brightest rays, she comprehended the meaning of these mysteries better than any other creature. Her life was therefore a continual prayer of meditation.

428. Is it necessary to add that it was also a continual prayer of

supplication, a perpetual jet of ejaculatory prayers, an unbroken chain of holy desires? She herself has revealed this great truth to us, when she declared that the Lord hath regarded the humility of his handmaid, and that he has filled with good things those that were hungry. Mary belonged to the first rank of these famished ones, who asked for the supersubstantial bread with incessantly renewed supplications. The life of Mary was a life of petition, of invocation, and of entreaty, continually addressed to Heaven, i.e. a veritable prayer of supplication.

429. Finally, all the prayers, desires, actions, and dispositions of Mary were summed up in the perfect conformity with the will of God: this was her last conclusion in everything: *Ecce ancilla Domini, fiat mihi secundum verbum tuum.* I am the handmaid of the Lord, I can have but one will, namely, that the will of God be fully accomplished in me. This is for her the term of all her wishes and the summit of perfection.

430. When a woman proclaimed the Mother of the Savior blessed, Jesus Christ replied: "*Quinimmo beati quiaudiunt verbum Dei et custodiunt illud!* Yea, rather blessed are they who hear the word of God and keep it!" (Luke XI, 28.) Our Lord wished to make us understand by this that the most holy Virgin was still more happy by her conformity to the will of God, by her supernatural union with God, than by her quality as Mother of the Savior. This union is much more real, intimate, and direct than that existing between the mother and her children: it comes nearest to the union which exists between the persons of the adorable Trinity; by it we are but one with God, as the Father, Son, and Holy Ghost are one. In whom was this union with God more perfect than in Mary? In her, it was the clear vision of Heaven, it was a perpetual contemplation and ecstasy.

431. Thus Mary is the model from which, as in a marvelous book, we learn the practice of perfect mental prayer, which consists in the prayer of faith and of the presence of God, in the prayer of meditation, of supplication, of union or conformity to the will of God. The prayer of Mary shall be the prayer of her children.

432. May it be thus, through thy intercession, O Mother of Divine

Grace! Art thou not thyself the book in which the most sublime, the most varied, and the most consoling subjects of meditation are developed? Art thou not the mirror in which he is reflected, who is Eternal Justice? Art thou not the Seat of Divine Wisdom, the singular Vessel of true devotion, the Ark of the covenant between Heaven and earth? Hail then, O Mother of divine meditation! "Hail, incomprehensible Book, in which we can read and study the Word, the eternal Son of the Father! *Ave, liber incomprehensus, quæ Verbum et Filium Patris mundo legendum exhibuisti.*" (St. Epiphanius.)

21

A LAST WORD OF THE GUIDE

433. After having followed our indications thus far, listen still, dear friend, to these last words of your Guide. Be a man of prayer and meditation, and it will suffice. As long as you possess the means of prayer (during life we have this means always) and have recourse to it faithfully, nothing will be lost to you, nothing compromised, everything will be saved and repaired.

434. Mental prayer, such as we have just explained it, forms part not only of every true prayer but of every exercise of piety and, in some regard, of every act of supernatural life. Some other exercises, such as the Holy Sacrifice of the Mass and Holy Communion, surpass it in dignity; but mental prayer occupies the first place when we consider the role which it is called upon to take in the spiritual life. It is the fire by which charity is enkindled, the source from which we draw the spirit of piety; it constitutes the soul of all the exercises, vivifies them, increases their value, and salutary effects.

435. With mental prayer, all the exercises of piety are kept up and bear fruit; without it, they languish and remain barren. Even the frequent reception of the Sacraments, Holy Communion, Holy Mass, instructions, spiritual reading, the recitation of the Divine Office, vocal prayers, all may become, and, in fact, do become, in the course

of time, a mere act of routine, without value and efficacy, if you are not careful to unite with these exercises that which constitutes their life, soul, vigor, and fertility, if you do not bring to them the spirit of faith, the prayer of faith. Yes, if you leave aside the prayer of faith, everything will disappear and fall to ruin, and you will be lost.

436. On the contrary, should you have abandoned all the Christian practices, should you have contracted an inveterate habit of sin, or fallen into despair, you will infallibly rise again by the prayer of faith and remain unshaken by persevering in this holy exercise.

437. If the damned in hell could still pray, their cause would be gained, for God never resists the prayer of faith. What increases the torments of these unhappy creatures is that there is not one of them who is not obliged to give himself this crushing testimony: if I had prayed when I had the opportunity, I would not be here now; it is therefore my own fault.

438. The prayer of faith is a light, which dispels darkness and illusions; it delivers the soul from blindness, brings her back and keeps her on the paths of justice and of truth, and preserves in her sentiments of humility and confidence.

439. Mental prayer is a heavenly dew penetrating the heart, triumphing over every hardness, insensibility, and obstinate resistance to grace. It causes the heavenly fire, which inflames, embraces, and excites, to descend to the soul; thus it preserves her from all drowsiness, and unceasingly prompts her to works of piety.

440. Finally, the prayer of faith and of the presence of God, of meditation, of supplication, and of union with God in the same will, is that intimate intercourse, in which God communicates with his child by that word which has created all, and which nothing can resist, which enraptures, embraces, strengthens, and attracts all hearts. "This word," says St. Paul, "is living and effectual, and more penetrating than any two-edged sword; and reaching unto the division of the soul and the spirit, of the joints also, and the marrow, and is a discerner of the thoughts and intents of the heart." (Hebr. IV, 12.)

441. Let us then give free scope to our admiration by repeating with St. Augustine: *"Quid oratione præclarius;* what is there more

glorious than mental prayer? *Quid vitæ nostræ utilius;* what more useful to our life? *Quid animo dulcius;* what more delicious to the soul? *Quid in tota nostra religione sublimius;* what more excellent in our holy religion?"

442. Devote yourself frequently to mental prayer, because God wishes it thus, and wishes it in your own interest. Yes, he asks of you continually to have recourse to mental prayer, because it is the most useful exercise of piety, because none of its acts will remain unrewarded.

443. God has resolved to grant us everything on two conditions: 1) that we ask it of him; 2) that we renew this petition until we have obtained it.

444. It is out of love for us that God requires of us not only to pray, but to attain a certain measure in prayer. The nearer we come to this measure, the nearer we approach the fullness of graces. A Christian, a religious, a family, a community, a people, the Church, has, at a given moment, come so much nearer to perfection, as this measure of prayer is more closely reached. How beautiful is this role of prayer, and the role of those who devote themselves to prayer! They best understand and most efficaciously procure their personal interests, the interests of their natural or religious family, of their country, and those of Holy Church.

445. Apply yourself then, whoever you may be, to mental prayer, because you could do nothing better. Besides the reasons already given, each one has, moreover, such as are personal and special, secret or public.

446. If you are still young, devote yourself to mental prayer, because the good Master will receive you with predilection; he has hidden the mysterious and ineffable delights of mental prayer from the great, and revealed them to the little, humble, and simple souls. Childhood is the most favorable age for being initiated into the exercise of mental prayer.

447. If you are a young man, the wants are more immediate, and the love of our Lord is, for that reason, more urgent; mental prayer answers the aspirations and necessities of your heart; it alone can

satisfy its insatiable desires, strengthen it, and render it invulnerable.

448. If you have reached manhood, it is time to show yourself a perfect Christian and soldier of Jesus Christ, to make use of your greatest strength; now it is in mental prayer, that the Holy Ghost will nourish you with the bread of the strong, and will superabundantly diffuse in your soul the gifts whose germ you have received in confirmation. In everything you will acquire a superiority which will be an effect of the habit of mental prayer, and will be expressed by signs of wisdom, intelligence, counsel, fortitude, science, piety, and fear of God. If you are at leisure, you could not find a nobler employment of your time; if you are occupied with business, it is with greater reason that you must, in your timetable, reserve an inviolable part to meditation. Your individual worth will be doubled thereby, everything will go better, should you even be a statesman and leader of nations.

449. Are you already on the decline of life, or reduced to a kind of repose on account of your infirmities, it is so much easier for you to multiply the acts by which you fill up the required measure of prayer in order that the designs of divine Mercy may be fully accomplished on you and your own.

450. If God has called you to his immediate service by the sacerdotal or religious vocation, know that if you are a priest by ordination, you can be a good priest only by meditation; if you are a religious by the profession of vows, you can be a good religious only by the faithful exercise of meditation.

451. Satan has sworn to prevent you from becoming a man of meditation? Will he succeed? Will he have the last word? Vow in your turn that you will be, at any cost, a man of meditation, and even become an apostle of meditation. To teach mental prayer, to recommend it, and to facilitate its practice is perhaps the best means of triumphing over the attacks of the demon and of becoming a master in this divine art.

452. Acknowledge that up to this day you have not sufficiently understood the necessity, facility, excellence, and advantages of mental prayer. Continue to improve in this doctrine by the very exer-

cise of meditation under the conduct of your Guide. Never abandon this Guide, consult it daily, follow it faithfully; soon you will perceive, to your satisfaction, that under this direction, your love and esteem for the practice of mental prayer will increase day by day.

453. Finally, whoever you may be, my dear friend, listen to this last word of mine: if you are a man of prayer, give thanks to God for this inestimable gift; if you are not yet a man of prayer, neglect nothing to become it very soon. "*Oportet semper orare et non deficere;* pray continually, and never be discouraged." (Luke XVIII, 1.) Let it be so, and it will suffice.

May the Father, Son, and Holy Ghost be glorified in all places by the Immaculate Virgin Mary.

22

FORMULAS FOR THE PROXIMATE PREPARATION

The object of the formulas in this appendix is to aid in producing the acts of the immediate preparation; they are not the acts themselves, and cannot replace them: it would not suffice then merely to read these formulas. They serve to guide the soul and suggest to her what to think and what is to be done by herself. You will, therefore, read them again, or consult your memory to know whether you have learned them by heart. It is not necessary, at each meditation, explicitly to make all the acts, whose formulas are given here, because all are implicitly comprised in one another. You will, therefore, select at one time this act, at another time a different one; never, however, will you omit the act of faith in the presence of God, and the act of adoration. The résumé of these formulas shows you how to shorten the time devoted to these acts, as circumstances may require. When mental prayer is combined with another exercise of piety, it is sometimes necessary still more to abridge and to omit parts of this résumé.

Act of Faith.

O my God, I believe all that thou hast taught and revealed, because thou art truth itself. In particular, do I believe that every word of thine, every maxim of thy Gospel, every truth taught by thy Holy Church, merits greater attention than all the teachings of men, and all the science of this world. Thou dost vouchsafe, in this hour, to call me to the holy exercise of prayer in order to speak to me. I hasten to come, because thou alone hast the words of eternal life. Speak then, Lord, for thy servant heareth. I believe in thy word, but increase this commencement of a belief, that this meditation may truly be a meditation of faith, and that my life may more and more become a life of faith.

Act of Faith in the Presence of God.

O my God, I firmly believe all that thou hast taught and revealed. I do, in particular, believe that thou art here present. I stand here in thy presence, as if I were alone in the world. My guardian angel, as well as my Rule, says to me: "*Magister adest et vocat te; the Master is here, and calls thee.*" Thou really dost, in this very moment, look down upon me with benevolence: thou sayest to me, as to the blind man of Jericho: What wilt thou that I should do to thee? — Lord, that I may see; open the eyes of my soul, that I may, without ceasing, behold and glorify thee during this exercise, and during my whole life.

Act of Adoration.

O my God, I firmly believe all that thou hast taught and revealed. I do, in particular, believe that thou art the Creator and absolute Master of all things. My first duty, in appearing before thy Majesty, is to prostrate myself before thee, thus acknowledging and affirming thy sovereign dominion over myself and all creatures. Glory, honor, love, and submission to the King of Heaven always and everywhere! During this audience, I unite my adoration and homage to those of Our Lord Jesus Christ, of the Blessed Virgin, of the whole heavenly Court, of the souls in Purgatory, of all the faithful living on earth, and especially of my fellow-brothers, who surround me: "*Benedicamus Patrem et Filium cum Sancto Spiritu, laudemus et superexaltemus eum in sæcula!* Let us bless the Father and the Son with the Holy Ghost; let us praise and exalt them during all ages!"

Act of Humility.

O my God, I firmly believe all that thou hast taught and revealed. I do, in particular, believe this word thou dost address to me: "Without me you can do nothing." Yes, I confess it, O my God, that without thee, I am nothing, I have nothing, I can do nothing; I can not even pronounce thy adorable name, nor conceive one good thought. I will therefore not be able to do anything during this meditation if thou dost not come to my assistance, if thou dost not vouchsafe to suggest to me what I should say, and to do with me what thou dost expect of me. Send me then thy Spirit, that he may assist my weakness, for of myself I know neither what to ask, nor how to pray. (Rom. VIII, 26.)

Act of Contrition.

O my God, I firmly believe all that thou hast taught and revealed. I do believe, in particular, that sin is the greatest injury that could be done to thy Majesty, and the greatest misfortune that could befall man. This misfortune is mine. Alas! I have numberless times wretchedly offended thee; I am an ungrateful, a miserable man, a vile sinner. I am a rebel who does not deserve to be admitted into the presence of thy Majesty. And still thou hast the goodness to call back to thee thy lost child. Be thou eternally blessed. I deplore my errors in the bitterness of my soul. Forgive me as I forgive those who have offended me; and teach me, in this holy exercise, to expiate my past faults, and no more to relapse in future.

Act of Thanksgiving.

O my God, I firmly believe all that thou hast taught and revealed. I believe, in particular, that it is to thee I owe all the good that is in me: existence, life, faith, vocation, the repeated forgiveness of my sins, the numberless gifts that are dependent on these first benefits; for me thou didst come into the world, thou didst suffer, die, and dost still live in our midst in the Holy Eucharist. The grace of this meditation is a new gift, surpassing all perishable goods. How can I worthily thank thee for so much goodness, I who am nothing but dust and ashes? At least, I wish to unite my thanksgiving to all those that have been rendered to thee since the beginning of the world, and to all those that will be rendered to thee during all eternity, repeating during my whole life, but especially during this meditation: "*Gratias agamus Domino Deo nostro. Dignum et justum est. Vere dignum et justum est......*"

Act of Invocation.

O my God, I believe all that thou hast taught and revealed. I believe especially in the truth of that word thou dost address to me: "Ask, and you shall receive; seek, and you shall find; knock, and it shall be opened to you." This is for me something more than an invitation; it is a command. Therefore, I come to thee in all simplicity to expose my petitions during this meditation. My confidence is entire and unshaken; because it rests, not on myself, but on thy word which cannot pass away. Grant me then all I need worthily to converse with thee; captivate my attention, enlighten my intellect, enliven my heart, direct and strengthen my will, that I may draw from this meditation all the fruits thou hast in thy mercy decreed to bestow on me; grant me the grace to learn to know thee better, to love thee more fervently, and to serve thee more faithfully. Amen.

Summary of the Preceding Acts.

O my God, thou dost call me in order to speak to me. Eagerly I come, because I firmly believe that thou alone hast the words of eternal life. Every word thou dost address to me is worth more than all the teachings of men. Thou art here present and dost look down upon me with benevolence. My first duty is to prostrate myself in thy presence to adore thee, by uniting my adorations with those of the whole heavenly Court. But who am I, O God, to dare to appear before thee? Without thee, I am nothing, I cannot conceive one good thought. Once more, what am I, O my God! Alas! I am less than nothing, because I have offended thee. Nevertheless, thou dost condescend again to receive thy prodigal child. Forgive me, O Lord, and teach me in future to relapse no more. Be thou unceasingly blessed and thanked, because thou hast forgiven me and still dost bestow new favors upon me. Teach me, in this meditation, to detest sin more and more, and to know thee better, O my God, to love thee more ardently, and to serve thee more faithfully. Amen.

23

OTHER FORMULAS OR MODELS WHICH MAY SERVE TO PRODUCE THE ACTS OF THE PROXIMATE PREPARATION

I. BEFORE THE PROSTRATION.

Invocation of the Guardian Angel.

Angel Guardian, thou who beholdest unceasingly the countenance of the Lord, who always standest in his holy presence! Faith teaches me that thou art given to me as my light, my guide, and my helper; assist me in the interview that I am about to have with my God.

Invocation of the Blessed Virgin.

O Mary, my good and tender Mother, who dist continually ponder in thy heart the words of Jesus, whose life has been an uninterrupted prayer! Assist me in acquitting myself of this holy exercise conformably to thy desire and to that of thy divine Son.

Act of Faith in the Presence of God.

O my God, I firmly believe that thou art here present, that thou dost penetrate my whole being. I am before thee as if I were alone in this world. Thou dost see and hear me, and thou knowest my most secret thoughts.

If the Meditation be made before the Blessed Sacrament, the following is to be added: O my God, I believe that thou art really present in the Most Holy Sacrament, and that from the tabernacle thou dost actually direct towards me the same regards of tenderness which during thy mortal life, thou didst so mercifully cast upon thy disciples, and even upon sinners.

II. During the Prostration.

Act of Adoration.

Prostrate before thy infinite Majesty, I adore thee, O my God, as my Creator and sovereign Lord of all things. I acknowledge with delight thy supreme dominion over me and all creatures. Glory, honor, love, and submission be to thee, the King of Heaven, at all times, and in all places! During this audience, I unite my adoration and homage with those of our Lord Jesus Christ, of the Blessed Virgin, of all the heavenly Court, of the souls in purgatory, of all the faithful upon earth, and in particular with those of the Brothers here present.

If the Meditation be made before the Blessed Sacrament, the following is to be added: I adore thee, O Jesus, present in the Holy Eucharist; I acknowledge thee as my Savior and sovereign Lord. In union with the Angels and Saints surrounding thy throne of mercy, I exclaim: "Praise and adoration forever be to Jesus in the Most Holy Sacrament!"

III. After the Prostration.

Act of Humility.

But who am I, O my God, that I dare to appear before thee? Thou art all, and I am but nothingness and weakness. I have nothing of my own, but my infidelities. Without thee, I cannot so much as conceive a good thought.

Act of Contrition.

O Jesus, my Savior, who didst die on the Cross to atone for my sins, I deplore my waywardness in the bitterness of my soul. Have mercy on me and pardon my ingratitude; deign to apply to my soul the merits of thy holy Passion; grant that I may learn, in this meditation, never more to relapse into sin in order that I may obtain mercy on the day of judgment.

Act of Thanksgiving.

I thank thee, O my God, for all graces and benefits, thou hast bestowed on me until this day. I thank thee particularly for my vocation, and for the singular favor thou dost presently grant me in admitting me to this celestial interview.

Act of Invocation.

O my God, thou didst command me to call thee by the sweet name of *Father*. I come therefore, O Father, to ask of thee, with the most child-like confidence, whatever is necessary to converse worthily with thee during this meditation. Captivate my attention, enlighten my understanding, inflame my heart, direct and strengthen my will, that I may lose none of the fruits thou dost intend to bestow upon me during this holy exercise.

Act of Union with our Lord.

O my Savior, I wish to perform this holy exercise with the intentions and dispositions thou didst have when praying to thy heavenly Father during thy mortal life, and which thou hast still now whilst praying in our holy Tabernacles. Thou art the head, and I am a member of thy mystical body. Meditate, I beseech thee, by this member, however unworthy it be; speak to our heavenly Father and ask of him, through me and for me, whatever is actually most necessary and useful to my soul. Amen.

24

BODY OF MENTAL PRAYER

Questions or Processes Which May Serve To Produce the Ordinary Acts During the Exercise of Mental Prayer.

The processes we have indicated are employed whenever we wish to study an object we have before us or in our mind. In mental prayer, they teach us to consider the object successively in all its parts, from all sides, and to discover in the primitive idea secondary ideas naturally connected therewith. The questions addressed to our faith and reason lead naturally to answers which ought to be given; they are like marks which the soul consults whenever she is overtaken by distractions, or they are like collections, whence the soul may draw thoughts whenever she feels powerless or dry. It is often useful to have the table of these questions before oneself during meditation; for certain minds, it is the most effectual means of retaining or bringing back the attention to the subject of mental prayer in moments of trouble and agitation. We repeat here what has been said when it was a question of the acts of preparation; it is not necessary, it is not even always possible, that about every truth, fact, or point, we put the entire series of questions enumerated in the table. What is essential is that the soul, by means of these questions, finds wherewith to occupy herself and that she does not herself open the door for strange thoughts. As to the manner of passing from the questions to the answers, and thus to the considerations, affections, and resolutions, we refer you to the directions of the Guide; the table of contents permits each one to find with the greatest facility the information which he desires. We likewise refer to the Guide those who would be sometimes embarrassed about the choice of a subject for mental prayer. We, however, think it not useless to sum up here, in a table, the directions interspersed throughout the Guide.

Questions for Mental Prayer.

1. Who said or did this? - For whom? - For what purpose?

2. What lesson should I learn from this truth or this fact? - What is its significance, its extent? - What are its practical consequences?

3. Do I adhere to this teaching? - Was it the rule of my appreciations and conduct in the past? - Am I even now disposed to take it for the rule of my conduct?

4. How did our Savior, the Blessed Virgin, and the saints think and act with regard to this? - What difference exists between their conduct and mine? - Why?

5. What does our Lord ask of me on this subject? - With what right does he make this demand (as our Creator, Redeemer, Master, Father, Friend, etc.)? What does the Blessed Virgin ask of me? - With what right?

6. Is it not wise, honorable, advantageous, and necessary for me to do that which God and the Blessed Virgin ask? - Is it not foolish, etc. to refuse?

7. Lastly, what must I practice or reform at once? - What would a damned soul do, what would it advise me to do in regard to this, if it could return to this world? - A saint? - What should I wish to have done at the hour of my death?

Advice.

You will put to yourself or repeat these questions several times, or some of these questions, proper to each point, truth, or event about which you are going to meditate. You will easily modify the form of these questions, if necessary, according as the object is an event, a truth, maxim, etc. When the question has been put, the answer presents itself, as it were, spontaneously; it rests on faith, on reason, on the testimony of men, on experience, etc. Pause at each answer, that it may penetrate your soul; to this end: 1) multiply the acts of faith on this answer; 2) animate yourself, according to the case, with sentiments of sorrow, of firm purpose, of gratitude, of admiration, etc.; 3) give utterance to these sentiments, and make use of the direct discourse when speaking to God, to our Lord, to the most blessed Virgin, to the saints; 4) above all, pray, invoke, supplicate, etc.

Texts or Subjects of Meditation.

1. The doctrines of the saints on mental prayer, reproduced in the Guide. Nearly all the chapters of the Guide, and the third chapter especially, furnish numerous texts for meditation. The table of contents permits you to choose a subject according to the needs of your soul.

2. The ordinary prayers of the Christian; and among these principally the *Pater,* the *Ave,* and, above all, the *Credo.* (See Guide, arts. 403-418.)

3. The hymn *Veni Creator,* the prose *Veni Sancte Spiritus,* and the invocation *Veni Sancte.*

4. The acts of faith, hope, charity, contrition, oblation, adoration, thanksgiving, etc.; the *Gloria Patri.*

5. The acts that are made before and after Communion.

6. The prayers of the Mass.

7. The mysteries of our holy Religion, particularly the mysteries of the Holy Rosary, the other mysteries of the life of our Savior, of the

Blessed Virgin, of the saints, and, above all, the Passion, the Holy Eucharist, and the Sacred Heart.

8. The litany of the most Holy Name of Jesus.

9. The litany of the most Holy Virgin, the *Ave Maris Stella,* the *Magnificat,* the *Salve Regina,* the *Memorare,* the *Sub Tuum,* and the other antiphons in honor of the Immaculate Virgin.

10. The litany of All Saints, and particularly the invocations that terminate it.

11. Holy Writ; of the Old Testament, the Psalms, and some biblical histories; of the New Testament, the Sermon on the Mount (Matt. V-VII), Our Lord's discourse after the Last Supper (St. John XIII-XVIII), the parables, such as that of the Prodigal Son (Luke XV), of the Pharisee and the Publican (Luke XVIII).

12. The Imitation of Christ, the Spiritual Combat, the writings of St. Alphonsus Liguori, etc.

13. For priests, the prayers of the ordination, in the Manual of the Ordinations.

14. For religious, the formula of their religious profession, their Rules.

15. Lastly, for all, the prayers of the Ritual for administering Baptism, Confirmation, Extreme Unction, and the prayers for the agonizing; finally, the prayers and the Office for the Dead.

25

CONCLUSION OF MENTAL PRAYER

Formulas or Models of Some Acts Which Ordinarily Form the Conclusion of Meditation.

What has been said of the formulas of the introduction, applies without reserve to the formulas of the conclusion. Among the acts of the conclusion is the renewal of the firm purpose. Every good resolution should be: 1. precise; 2. personal; 3. immediate; 4. firm; 5. constant. (See Guide, 263-268.)

Act of Thanksgiving.

O my God! I thank thee for the audience with which thou hast honored me; I thank thee for all the lights and good sentiments thou hast imparted to me, and for all the good resolutions thou hast suggested to me.

Act of Regret.

O my God! I ask pardon for all the carelessness of which I have made myself guilty during this holy exercise. I profoundly humble myself on their account. Have mercy on me, O my God, and do not permit that my negligence deprives me of the graces thy goodness had prepared for me.

Renewal of Firm Purpose.

O my God! I renew, with better determination than ever, the resolution of...; and in order to be faithful to it, I will adopt the following means....

Spiritual Bouquet.

For my spiritual bouquet, I shall take these words... I will often repeat them during the day and especially on this or that occasion.

Colloquy.

O my God! Bless again this resolution before I withdraw, that I may constantly remain faithful to it. Dearest Virgin Mary, my good and tender Mother, into thy hands I deposit the fruits of this meditation as also my other spiritual goods; preserve and increase them, that thy child may become less unworthy of thee. St.........., obtain for me the grace of fidelity to my resolution. Dear Guardian Angel, remove far from me every cause of dissipation, which would expose me to lose the fruits of my meditation.

26

ANALYTICAL TABLE OF CONTENTS

CHAPTER ONE

What the Guide proposes to itself and to whom it is addressed.
1. The Guide offers its counsels to those who wish to learn to make mental prayer. — 2. Is a Guide necessary to pray well? — 3. Are there not many simple and upright souls who, without a method, have succeeded in making excellent meditations? — 4. God wishes that in order to attain an object, we should make use of the means which lead to it; this principle applies to meditation. — 5. It is one thing to make meditation in certain circumstances; it is a different thing to make it in a regular manner, at determined hours. — 6. Regular meditation is like an art which has its method. — 7. This method is the ensemble of rules which facilitate the exercise of meditation. — 8. The Guide insists more than the ordinary methods upon the excellence, the advantages, and the facility of meditation, so that this exercise may be loved and esteemed. — 9. It tries to lay open in a simple manner the teachings of the saints on this subject. — 10. On this account, it avoids in the exposition whatever has the appearance of a scientific treatise. — 11. It likewise removes whatever might appear complicated in the classification. — 12. It is distinguished by

the stress it lays on the role of faith in the exercise of mental prayer. — 13. No one has spoken more highly of this role of faith than our Divine Master. — 14. The Apostles, and especially St. Paul, were the faithful echoes of our Lord. — 15. Every method speaks of the connection between prayer and faith; no one insists on it more strongly than we propose to do. — 16. The spirit of faith alone can make the exercise of mental prayer possible. — 17. A good will is the only condition for succeeding in mental prayer. — 18. To obtain this good will, it suffices to ask it of God. — 19 & 20. The Guide is addressed especially to generous young men, Christian mothers, earnest fathers, religious souls, and priests. — 21. What progress would you already have made if you had always applied yourself diligently to meditation? — 22. You will be a man of mental prayer if you never cease to wish it. — 23. It is never too late but always urgent to give yourself to it. — 24. Say therefore: "I shall become a man of meditation because I will it." — 25. There will be question of that kind of mental prayer only, in which all can succeed.

CHAPTER TWO

In what prayer essentially consists.

26. — What distinguishes mental prayer from vocal prayer. — Mental prayer considered as a regular exercise. — Facility of this exercise. 26. Prayer is an act by which we elevate our soul towards God. — 27. It is an act of piety and humility, by which the soul turns towards God. (St. Augustine.) — 28. This act may be a simple thought, a remembrance, desire, etc. — 29. Prolonged more or less, it becomes a conversation with God. — 30. Prayer depends on the virtue of religion. — 31. It is peculiar to prayer that it honors God, by the request or expectation of some favors. — 32. Difference between mental and vocal prayer. — 33. Better to understand this difference, we must not stop at the etymology; it is not the articulated word and the tone of voice that distinguishes it from the other. — 34. Mental prayer can be made even in a loud voice. — 35. In mental prayer the soul speaks to God without making use of previously prepared formulas. — 36. In

tions of the Rule concerning mental prayer relate to its time, place, duration, frequency, and some other details. — 65. Considered as an exercise of the Rule, mental prayer changes neither in nature nor form, nor in its object. — 66. Definition of mental prayer, considered as a regular exercise. — 67. The object of mental prayer is, therefore, to conduct us to our end, i.e. to make us know, love, and serve God, and thus obtain everlasting life.

CHAPTER THREE

That mental prayer takes the first rank among religious exercises.

68. The better you know the excellence and advantages of meditation, the more you will apply yourself to it. — 69. We collect here what the saints have told us on this point; these maxims are excellent subjects of meditation or of the mixed mental prayer. — 70. The spiritual exercises should be the privileged creditors. 71. Mental prayer is the shortest road to perfection. (St. Ignatius.) — 72. As a fish cannot live out of the water, so a Christian cannot live without prayer. (St. Augustine.) — 73. Pray, pray, pray, and above all, recommend prayer. (St. Alphonsus Liguori.) — 74. Without the exercise of mental prayer, we know neither what we are and do, nor what we have to fear. (idem.) — 75. Without prayer, no salvation; without meditation, no prayer. (idem.) — 76. If we devote ourselves to meditation, we cannot persevere in sin. (idem.) — 77. It is the spirit of mental prayer that the demon most fears and seeks to destroy in souls. (St. Philip Neri.) — 78. Mental prayer cures lukewarmness; — 79. saves from hell; — 80. is the common source of all virtues. (St. Vincent de Paul, St. Augustine, St. Teresa.) — 81. He who is not a man of mental prayer will never arrive at a high degree of sanctity. (St. Aloysius Gonzaga.) — 82. Mental prayer comprises the exercise of every virtue. (Suarez.) — 83. God gives his choice graces to men of meditation only. Example of St. Francis of Assisi. — 84. Mental prayer makes the soul fit to receive the impressions of grace. (St. Francis de Sales.) — 85. Everything may be wanting to us; but if we preserve the practice of mental prayer, it

manner in which we acquit ourselves of the exercises of piety, on the life of our Savior and of the saints. — 108. It is also useful to conform to the mysteries honored by Holy Church, and to the feasts celebrated by her. — 109. The meditation books may be of great use, but we ought not servilely to confine ourselves to them. — 110. The choice of the subject depends on the disposition of those who make meditation. The masters of the spiritual life distinguish three states in the Christian life: the state of the beginners, that of the intermediate, and that of the perfect. — 111. The beginners are those who endeavor to despoil themselves of the old man; subjects of meditation suitable to them. — 112. The intermediate are those who seek to clothe themselves with Jesus Christ by the imitation of his virtues: subjects suitable to them. — 113. The perfect are those who endeavor to unite themselves more and more intimately with God by the thought of his presence, the purity of their intention, and their conformity to his holy will: subjects suitable to them. 114. These three states are called the purgative, the illuminative, and the unitive way. It must, however, be remarked that this distinction is not at all absolute. — 115. Punctuality for the time of the audience. — 116. The hours most favorable to mental prayer are in the morning and evening. — 117. Mental prayer considered as an exercise of the Rule should, as much as possible, be made in community. — 118. When the saints were prevented from retiring into solitude, they knew how to be recollected and to pray in the midst of tumult. — 119. The indispensable condition for praying well is solitude of the heart. — 120. But according to the testimony of our Savior, the proper place, or the house of prayer, is the church, the chapel, or oratory.

CHAPTER SIX

What is to be done at the beginning of mental prayer? Or in what the immediate preparation for the "prayer of faith and of the presence of God" consists.

121. The various acts which form the immediate preparation. — 122. Invocation of the Holy Ghost and the most holy Virgin. — 123.

ence of God, and this suffices. *(Idem.)* — 151. It may even prove to our greater advantage not to be able to say anything. *(Idem.)* — 152. We should esteem ourselves happy to be allowed to figure before our Lord as a statue. *(Idem.)* — 153. Mary Magdalen said nothing when sitting at the feet of Jesus and weeping over her sins; the Blessed Virgin, by the Cross, did not speak a word. Does not the greatest happiness of the angels consist in enjoying the presence of God? — 154. Do not therefore fear to remain at the prayer of faith and of God's presence; it is an excellent prayer. — 155. Repeat then, with the angels, the words of the *Preface* and *Sanctus* of the Mass. Could you do anything better than what the angels are doing? — 156. If these acts of faith in the presence of God are prolonged to the close of mental prayer, be nowise troubled about it. — 157. Before the most holy Sacrament, the act of faith in the presence of God takes a special character. — 158. If, then, you taste the sweetness of the presence of God, go no farther. — 159. This manner of meditation is an act, or rather a series of interior acts, and not a state of indifference and idleness. — 160. Do you wish to be preserved from illusion? Examine into the fruits of your meditation. — 161. As to the exterior deportment, he who takes part in a public service ought to conform to the liturgical prescriptions; he who prays in private is guided by respect towards Almighty God; he who is a member of a community conforms to established usage. — 162. The attitude of the body greatly influences the sentiments of the soul. (St. Augustine.) — 163. Thoughts of St. Francis de Sales on this point: we should pray always with respect. — 164. We must pray with our whole being. — 165. Our Lord is a model for us in this matter.

CHAPTER SEVEN

In what the principal part, called the body of meditation consists, and how the subject of meditation is naturally divided into several points.

166. How the subject is exposed. — 167. *First* and *second prelude.* — 168. The object is a truth, a fact or mixed subject. — 169. In our explanations, it is generally understood that the subject is a truth. — 170.

In order to grasp the subject better, the attention is successively drawn, first to one point, then to another, etc.; hence, the division of the subject into several points. 171. Meditation books generally present the subject as divided into several points, but you must not consider yourself restricted by them. — 172. Besides, the points to which we should adhere in the same subject vary according to circumstances. — 173. The soul applies her faculties variously according to the nature of the subject and the object she proposes to herself. — 174. All the faculties of the soul have reference to these three principal ones: the intellect (understanding, mind), the sensibility (heart), and the will. When the soul operates, she applies all or one of her faculties to the object she has in view. — 175. Mental prayer is such a complicated operation that all the faculties of the soul find occasion to work at it. — 176. In ascetic language, the acts of the intellect, heart, and will, take respectively the names of considerations, affections, and resolutions. 177. These three kinds of operations are ranged in the order we have observed, but this arrangement must neither be rigorously nor exclusively adhered to in practice.

CHAPTER EIGHT

How to make the "considerations," and in what the "prayer of meditation" consists.

178. The considerations form the chief matter of the prayer of meditation. — 179 & 180. Why we ought especially to meditate on the truths of faith. — 181. We must, however, not neglect the light of reason. — 182. Meditation, or considerations, are always useful, and often necessary, especially when made on the main truths of our religion. — 183. For want of reflection, man does not know himself. — 184. He does not know God. — 185. He does not appreciate his character as a child of God. — 186. Jesus Christ is neither known nor listened to. — 187. The Gospel is neither known nor appreciated. — 188. Sin is not feared, and worldly maxims are followed. — 189. Our conduct is most frequently absurd. — 190. It will be too late one day to make these considerations, and to say: *Ergo erravimus.* — 191. One

single truth constantly meditated on would suffice to lead us to our end. — 192. Why do so many persons allow themselves to be dragged along by the current of opinions? Because they do not reflect. — 193. Without meditation, we can be neither men nor Christians. — 194. But is it easy to meditate, to make considerations? — 195. The least cultivated intelligence can do what God requires in meditation. — 196. Example of St. Felix of Cantalice. — 197. You are asked to do in meditation only what you already do in intellectual labor. — 193. Consider, then, the proposed truth, with the eyes of faith and reason. — 199. If you can go no farther, this suffices; but often it will be easy for you to prolong and vary your considerations. — 200. Study the life of our Lord, of the blessed Virgin and the saints. — 201. Lay stress on the motives which you have for practicing virtue. — 202. Especially take practical resolutions and examine your present dispositions, your past dispositions, anticipate the future, for true meditation must teach you to know yourselves and to become such as God wishes you to be. — 206. Besides, there are rules for your direction, collections, from which to draw the developments. — 207. There are questions which we may put to ourselves before each object: *quis quid* etc. — 208. The answers to these and similar questions constitute the considerations. — 209. Outside of the ordinary resources, we can, in this part of mental prayer, dispose of all God has revealed to us: what a vast field! — 210. It is always easy to consult God and receive an answer from him. — 211. God does not want us to neglect human means, the intellectual labor. — 212. Yet without God we can do nothing. — 213. Hence the necessity of having recourse to God by frequent invocations. — 214. When we humbly acknowledge that God gives the understanding, we always succeed in making considerations. — 215. Do not confound meditation with the study of the subject. — 216. Be not solicitous for great thoughts and sublime ideas. — 217. Therefore, courage and confidence.

CHAPTER NINE

How the affections are produced, and in what the prayer of supplication consists.

218. In every well-made meditation, the mind acts on the heart and produces affections. — 219. The name of affections is given to various emotions and inclinations of the soul. — 220. We distinguish spontaneous affections, and affections voluntary in their nature or causes. — 221 & 222. How the affections may vary. — 223. The affections are acts of humility and confidence, of renunciation and resignation, and especially acts of love. — 224. If the affections present themselves, they must not be stopped; thus the affections are added to the considerations, and the resolutions to the affections. (St. Francis de Sales.) — 225. Were they to take up the whole time, they should not be thrust back, *(idem.)* — 226. God speaks to us in the affections, and produces in us these diverse sentiments. (St. Vincent de Paul.) — 227. It is therefore not proper to oppose the action of God. — 228. There are, however, sensible affections which we must distrust. — 229. Certain sensible attractions are graces. — 230. It is often necessary to strive to produce affections. — 231. We, of course, speak here of affections inasmuch as they depend on our will. — 232. One thing is always in our power, viz. the invocations, or prayer. — 233. In mental prayer, it is preferable to all else to make frequent petitions or requests. (St. Alphonsus Liguori.) — 234. Hence the principal fruit of mental prayer lies in the prayer of supplication, *(idem.)* 235. How consoling to state that the most useful act of meditation is also the most easy. — 236. Is there a condition in life in which this simple prayer is not easy? — 237. Adhere, therefore, on the advice of St. Alphonsus Liguori, to its practice. — 238. It is also the practice of Holy Church. — 239. Keep for your own use a collection, a spiritual quiver of ejaculatory prayers. — 240. Since God is present, take the habit of speaking directly to him. — 241. Some examples of direct invocations. — 242. In the Gospel, the considerations are short, the invocations vivid and frequent. — 243. Can it ever occur that you have nothing more to ask of God? — 244. How many subjects of urgent

supplication do you not find in yourself! — 245. Put no bounds to your petitions and desires. — 246. Increase your supplications in favor of all noble and holy works. — 247. Practice the apostolate of prayer; prayer obtains more than mere preaching. — 248. In the greatest abandonment, it is always easy to make acts of humility. — 249. The act of humility becomes easier, the weaker you are; therefore no excuse. — 250. The least act of humility during meditation is worth more than all the science of the world. (St. Teresa.) — 251. Practice of the Saints, especially of St. Francis of Assisi; example of David. — 252. Never fail to join confidence with humility, thereby you fall back on the prayer of supplication. — 253. Excellence of this kind of mental prayer. — 254. When the heart belongs to God, all belongs to him. — 255. The utility of mental prayer consists less in the meditation than in the affections, prayers, and resolutions.

CHAPTER TEN

How "resolutions" are formed, and in what the prayer of union consists.

256. The purposes and decisions of the will are called resolutions. — 257. The germs of the resolutions are already contained in the considerations and affections. — 258. God must act on the will, otherwise it is powerless. — 259. The action of the will is decisive and necessary. — 260. The resolution is a complete and the most personal act of mental prayer. — 261. We must not fail to devote some moments to it. — 262. That the resolutions may produce some fruits, they must be recommended to God and the most holy Virgin. — 263. That a resolution be good, it should be precise and determined, — 264 & 265, personal, — 266, immediate, or proximate, — 267, firm, — 268, persevering, or constantly renewed until satisfactory results be obtained. — 269. The principal quality is evidently the conformity to God's holy will. — 270. Hence all the parts of mental prayer verge to this conclusion, and all the kinds of prayer have their consummation in the prayer of union with the will of God. — 271. Union of grace is in proportion to the union of our will with the will of God. — 272. By the union of wills, we become completely the organs of Jesus Christ.

CHAPTER ELEVEN

CHAPTER TWELVE

bouquet; — 297. the colloquy. — 298. We ought to act like a man carrying great riches. (St. Francis de Sales.)— 299. We must, by some vocal prayers, recommend these spiritual riches to God, the most holy Virgin, and our protectors, and desire that the will of God be done in all things. — 300. Some formulas of these vocal prayers.

CHAPTER THIRTEEN

How to proceed, when the subject of the meditation is a fact, instead of a truth.

301. The subject of mental prayer may be either a fact or a mixed subject. — 302. The actions and words of our Lord nearly always constitute a mixed subject. — 303 & 304. The considerations, affections, and resolutions are pretty nearly the same, as when we meditate on a truth.

CHAPTER FOURTEEN

How to proceed in the exercise called mixed mental prayer.

305. Mixed mental prayer is at once vocal and mental. — 306. The subject is chosen from a book, or it is some vocal prayer. — 307. We read a passage, or pass over in our mind some portion of the prayer, and proceed with the considerations, affections, and resolutions as indicated above. — 308. Then we proceed to a second thought, and do the same again. — 309. St. Francis de Sales strongly recommends this kind of meditation; — 310. likewise St. Alphonsus Liguori and St. Philip Neri. — 311. Avoid changing meditation into reading. — 312. There is a difference between meditation and spiritual reading; — 313. we must not therefore simply read instead of meditating.

CHAPTER FIFTEEN

How mental prayer may be combined with other exercises of piety.

314. Mental prayer may be made in the form of the various exercises of piety. — 315. The preparation is made according to the indi-

cated form, but more briefly; — 316, likewise the considerations, affections, and resolutions. — 317. Let us take some examples: Benediction with the Blessed Sacrament; how much does the presence of our Lord facilitate the acts of meditation! — 318. We converse directly with him. — 319. The visit to the Blessed Sacrament is, by nature, a divine audience and an excellent meditation. — 320. Can a more moving subject be found than the Way of the Cross? — 321. You may make use of a book, but make, above all, personal reflections. — 322. It is here especially that you should address to yourself the questions indicated in art. 207. — 323. An instruction, a conference, is equally favorable to the acts of mental prayer. — 324. Holy Mass is, in its essence, an excellent subject of meditation. — 325. In the sacrifice of the Mass, Jesus himself prays for us on the altar. — 326. We cannot, at that time, ask too much of him. — 327. Meditation gives us a penetration into this *mystery of faith.* — 328 & 329. But the incomparable mental prayer is Holy Communion. — 330. In this kind of meditation, it is important to make the acts of the conclusion.

CHAPTER SIXTEEN

How and why the examination of mental prayer is made.

331. The examination of mental prayer is, in some way, a part of the exercise. — 332. This examination is the shortest way to arrive at making mental prayer well. — 333. It is necessary to fix a moment for that exercise. — 334. You will ask your guardian angel to assist you. — 335. The examination should embrace all the parts of mental prayer: — 336. the preparation, the considerations, the affections, the resolutions, especially the particular, or principal resolution. — 337. It is very useful to make a diligent search of the ordinary defects of our meditations; — 338. to impose a penance on oneself for every meditation badly made; — 339. to keep an account of our mental prayer. — 340 & 341. Résumé of questions for the examination of mental prayer.

CHAPTER SEVENTEEN

Why God permits us to encounter difficulties during mental prayer. — Which are the ordinary difficulties and how we can triumph over them.

342. To be complete, there remains a word to be said about difficulties; — 343. for mental prayer has its difficulties, not only because it is a labor, — 344. but particularly, because the devil wants to hinder us from performing mental prayer. — 345. He attacks us on our weak side. — 346. These difficulties are, like all temptations, inevitable and useful; — 347. above all, to keep us in humility. — 348. There are three kinds of obstacles or difficulties: distractions, dryness, and illusions. — 349. A distraction is a want of attention in the soul to the subject which should occupy her. — 350. Distractions are voluntary or involuntary; the latter are neither guilty nor injurious. — 351. They may be voluntary either directly or indirectly. — 352. They are not voluntary, if, from the beginning, we direct our intention towards making a good meditation. (St. Thomas.) — 353. Dissipation of the mind is the most common cause of our distractions. — 354. In this state, the soul is unable to recollect herself, to reflect. (Parable of the sower.) — 355. We must combat dissipation in its causes. — 356. We must, above all, guard against infractions of silence. — 357. To remove these causes is to effect the disappearance of most of the distractions. 358. Still, some of them will remain. — 359. We are not responsible for these distractions as long as we are not aware of them. — 360. Battle is victory. — 361 & 362. Should even this struggle last the whole time, meditation would not thereby be defective; it is the meditation of patience, which is very useful. (St. Francis de Sales.) — 363. Make use even of some exterior means, such as looking at the tabernacle, taking a book, etc.; but, above all, have frequent recourse to faith. — 364. Never be discouraged; the prayer of supplication is always possible to you. — 365. Dryness or aridity is that state of the soul in which she finds herself unable to produce the acts of mental prayer. 366. Voluntary dryness is combated first by removing the causes, 367, then directly by acts of faith, humility, confidence, etc. — 368. Dryness may continue without any fault of ours; the greatest saints have passed

through this painful trial. — 369. In that case, we must not give way to discouragement; example of St. Teresa. — 370. In aridities, God tries those whom he loves. (St. Teresa.) — 371. In such state, look on yourself as a beggar in the presence of God and the saints. (St. Philip Neri.) — 372. We profit most in aridities. (St. Alphonsus Liguori.) — 373. As a mother refuses sugar to a sick child, thus God refuses the spiritual sweets to those whom they might injure. (St. Francis de Sales.) — 374. We may, nevertheless, sweetly complain to our Lord. *(idem.)* — 375. The soul that kept herself in the presence of God has been nourished with substantial food, and the object of meditation is attained. — 376. When the demon cannot otherwise divert us from meditation, he tries to draw us into illusions. — 377. A first illusion consists in our believing that we shall never make mental prayer well. — 378. A second one consists in our believing it useless to apply ourselves to mental prayer, since as yet we have not remarked any progress. — 379. If, with goodwill, we give ourselves to the practice of mental prayer, we shall always progress. (St. Francis de Sales.) — 380. Do not measure the fruit of your meditations by the consolations, but by the good desires which you feel. — 381. The resolutions are the great fruit of meditation. (St. Francis de Sales.) — 382. A third illusion is to believe ourselves advanced in virtue because we have experienced good sentiments during meditation. — 383. We are not under illusion if we are disposed to work seriously at our own reform; — 384. if we are charitable (St. Francis de Sales); — 385. if we mortify our self-love and passions (St. Ignatius of Loyola); — 386. if we wish what God wishes (St. John of the Cross); — 387. above all, if we are humble and obedient. — 388. Let us, therefore, be as little children in the hands of God.

CHAPTER EIGHTEEN

How we ought to endeavor to make our mental prayer a "prayer of faith."

389. We again lay stress on the role of faith; because faith is the principle, object, and instrument of every mental prayer. (Rev. Father Chaminade.) — 390. All the acts of mental prayer are either directly

or indirectly acts of faith. (Suarez.) — 391. Faith is the base and principle of every meditation; it alone can render meditation possible and easy. — 392. The livelier your faith, the easier will meditation become. — 393. Faith is also the instrument of mental prayer; — 394. the habitual medium of communication with God. — 395. It enlightens us about the truths on which we wish to meditate; — 396. it is the best means to obtain all from God; — 397. it puts us in relation with God and all his revelations to us. — 398. It is again from faith that we draw the dispositions necessary to meditate well. — 399. It is by faith that we commence the exercise of mental prayer and bring it to the highest perfection. — 400. By it we live in the supernatural regions. — 401. Faith is the common source of all virtues. — 402. The domain of faith, and consequently that of mental prayer, is immense. — 403. This domain is comprised in the Apostles' Creed. — 404. Father Chaminade advises us to choose our subjects of meditation from this symbol. 405. *Credo.* — 406-415. How we can meditate on the symbol of our faith. — 416. This symbol comprises everything in the order of nature and that of grace. — 417. It answers all the questions which interest humanity. — 418. It unrolls completely to our view the divine plan of the Creation and Redemption.

CHAPTER NINETEEN

How the Blessed Virgin is the patroness and the model of men of mental prayer.

419. The Blessed Virgin is the patroness and most perfect model of men of mental prayer. — 420. The best part was for her. — 421. Prayer is the most excellent thing we can do: examples of Jesus and Mary. — 422. The prayer of Mary had all the characters we have pointed out; — 423. it was a prayer of faith; — 424. her whole life was a life of faith. — 425. Her divine Son was pleased to exercise her faith. — 426. Her prayer was an exercise of the presence of God, — 427. of meditation, — 428. of supplication, — 429. of conformity to the will of God and of union with God. — 430. "Beati qui audiunt verbum Dei et custodiunt illud," applied to the most holy Virgin. — 431. Mary is

then the perfect model of mental prayer; may it be given us to resemble her. — 432. O Virgin Mary, obtain this grace for us!

CHAPTER TWENTY

A last word of the Guide.

433. Be men of mental prayer and it suffices. — 434. Mental prayer is the soul of every prayer. — 435. Without mental prayer, everything is done by routine — 436. Mental prayer can save everything. — 437. The reprobate are in hell only because they neglected prayer. — 438. The prayer of faith is a light which illuminates, 439. a celestial dew, which refreshes, a flame which warms the heart. — 440. In mental prayer, we speak to God and God speaks to us. — 441. Words of St. Augustine on the excellence of mental prayer. — 442. It is in our own interest that God wishes us to give ourselves to mental prayer. — 443. God wants to grant everything to us on condition that we ask it of him and never cease to ask. — 444. The more you pray, the more useful you will be to yourself and to others. — 445. Apply yourself then, whoever you may be, to mental prayer: — 446. if you are a child, because childhood is the age of innocence, the age of our Savior's predilection; — 447. if a young man, because your necessities are more immediate, — 448. if an adult, because it is at this age that you must show yourself a strong and perfect Christian, — 449. if an aged man, because you are more at leisure to pray that the will of God may be accomplished in you, — 450. if a priest or religious, because you can neither be a good priest nor a good religious unless you practice mental prayer. — 451. The demon has sworn to prevent you from making mental prayer: will he be master? — 452. Have you, until this day, understood the necessity, facility, excellence, and advantages of mental prayer? — 453. *Oportet semper orare et non deficere;* may it be so.